Demography and Migration in Asia

Demography and Migration in Asia

Issues and Trends

Edited by
Anita Sengupta
Suchandana Chatterjee

Maulana Abul Kalam Azad Institute of Asian Studies, Kolkata

SHIPRA

ISBN: 978-81-7541-587-4

First Published in India in 2011

Demography and Migration in Asia

Published by:
SHIPRA PUBLICATIONS
H.O.: LG 18-19, Pankaj Central Market, Patparganj,
I.P. Ext., Delhi-110092, Tel: 91-11-2223 5152, 2223 6152
Br.Off.: 4617/18, Ansari Road, Darya Ganj,
New Delhi-110002, Tel: 6594 6453, 9810522367
E-mail: info@shiprapublications.com
www.shiprapublications.com

Contents

Introduction

Global migration has been assessed in both positive and negative terms. The inflow and outflow of human capital has far-reaching consequences and this has been reflected in the sensitivities of the communities who are involved. The literature on the migrants is varied—on the one hand a large volume of writings portrays 'the migrant question'. On the other hand, a significant volume of the literature reflects on the sensibilities of the migrants and their dilemmas of social adaptation. A very different category of writings emphasizes legal aspects of migration, the element of control of migrants through laws especially in the newly created SEZs of the Far East or India's eastern districts. These diverse trends are analyzed in both short-term and long-term historical perspectives and the locales of settlement have been emphasized. The profile of the migrant has also assumed great prominence.

Speaking about the patterns of migration in Siberia, Central Asia and India, authors in this volume have discussed related issues on these aspects and diverse migrant experiences. In continuation of the international seminar *Asiatic Russia, Central Asia and India-migration, regions, regionalism in historical perspective* that was held in Baikal,

Siberia from 19-21 July 2009, an international symposium *Demography and Migration in Asia-issues and trends* was held in Kolkata on February 24, 2010. This volume, based on the studies presented in the two symposiums, not only deals with migration as a specimen but also as a tool of interdisciplinary research. Demography, another related aspect of migration and the dispersal of population across the Asiatic borderlands is another focus. The intricacies in the Russian Far East have been compared with those of eastern and north-eastern regions of India.

B.V. Bazarov and N.I. Atanov examine new tendencies in East Asian geopolitics through an analysis of the ongoing process of economic regionalism in East Asia. They argue that a new form of Chinese regionalism is now evident which they refer to as "global regionalism", in the course of which the growing demand for raw materials will be satisfied with the help of neighbouring states. Chinese global regionalism is identified as a new Chinese global strategy. In this context the participation of China in the development of natural resources of East Siberia and the Far East, energy cooperation and cooperation in other spheres have been examined.

Homeswar Goswami examines the consequences of migration for Assam with particular reference to illegal migration from Bangladesh. He examines various categories of migrants both in the pre and post independence periods. In the post independence period the negative socio-economic and political consequences of Bangladeshi migration have been highlighted. The author argues that once immigrants arrive it is nearly impossible to deport them. He stresses stringent measures that are required to be undertaken to stop illegal infiltration.

In a similar vein, Jayanta Kumar Ray, in the course of examining the implications of regional migration for the East and North East of India argues that given the illegal nature of the migration it should be identified as 'infiltration' rather than migration. He argues that while accurate figures may be difficult to collect more or less dependable estimates are available that point to the large volume of this illegal movement. Stressing the need to underline the connections between infiltration and terrorism, he argues for the adoption of measures to prevent the situation from becoming a major security challenge for the state. Reflective of the situation in the Russian Far East, Ray predicts the possibilities of a demographic change that could be problematic in the future.

P.L. Dash analyzes and highlights a few important aspects of the population movement in Russia in general and Asiatic Russia in particular through the years following the demise of the Soviet Union. He underlines that compared to the more systematic patterns of movement in the Soviet years migration in the post Soviet era was less regularized. In certain cases as in Asiatic Russia this often resulted in the mass movement of people out of inhospitable terrains towards habitations that were more hospitable often without the knowledge of the state. Various types of migratory movements occurred. There was a spate of voluntary migration of groups who were non-ethnics and involuntary migration who were forced by rising ethnic sentiments. There were also other categories who moved in search of livelihood or because of changes in the legal sphere.

Gulnara Mendikulova in her paper on the problems and prospects of migration in post Soviet Central Asia refers to similar types of migration. While focusing on the Kazakh case she underlines the problems that illegal migration has caused particularly where the migrants have been involved with criminal activities. Both Mendikulova and Dash also focus on the criminalization of migrants and how this poses a problem for states. Dash also notes the specific situation prevailing in Tajikistan, as the only country that passed through the post-Soviet chaos of a civil war resulting from regional, factional rivalry, as deserving of special attention.

Nandini Bhattacharya focuses on one aspect of the problem when she writes about gender issues associated with migration in Tajikistan. She explains how migration acted as an easy answer to the present economic crisis, but in the process gave rise to a new set of problems with complex and prolonged effects on Tajik state and society. Women, who were mostly at the receiving end of the process, became victims of uncertainty and desertion. The solutions that have been sought for the problem have not been very reassuring. She notes that the role of migration as a 'social shock absorber' against poverty thus seems to have boomeranged into a number of deeper shocks that the Tajik society is destined to bear in future. For social sustenance and temporary economic relief, migration was a quick solution; but like any quick remedy it had effects that endangered the social foundations of the Tajik society in the long run.

Kamilla Sheryazdanova, therefore identifies migration as a 'factor of vulnerability' particularly in the context of integration of the region. She argues that one of the most critical problems before the post Soviet states is related to migration. In order to deal with the problems associated with migration it is necessary to adopt laws on fighting illegal migration and improve labour legislation, especially in the sphere of the foreign manpower import. It is also necessary to develop institutional base, to strengthen the potential in migration flows control, and to prevent illegal migration (opening new border outposts, strengthening the control over the arriving people).She argues that a significant role preventing illegal migration can be played by bilateral and multilateral agreements between the states and Russia and China.

Bhavna Dave examines the challenges of ethnic repatriation and labour migration in Kazakhstan. Her article draws attention to the enormous challenges that policies of ethnic repatriation encounters within a globalizing framework in which regional and transnational factors, rather than national policies dominates. Dave shows how efforts to boost its demographic base by bringing in Kazakh diaspora from neighbouring states of Central Asia as well as from Mongolia, Afghanistan, Iran, Iraq, Turkey, and China soon reached a saturation point as very few Kazakhs from outside of the CIS availed of the repatriation offer. She illustrates how Kazakhstan found it difficult to economically absorb and culturally integrate the diaspora returnees and how the separation between the titular Kazakhs and the returnees remains pronounced. Furthermore, as a result of the shared Soviet experience, the labour migrants from Central Asia fitted into Kazakhstani society more easily in cultural and social terms than the ethnic Kazakh returnees from outside the former Soviet republics. The problems encountered in the integration of the oralman into the fabric of Kazakhstani society and state apparatus is used to demonstrate that ethnic repatriation targets and policies are very difficult to achieve in the absence of a democratic notion of citizenship or a shared vision of national ideology.

The relationship between migration and demography is complex. Vastly differing population growth rates, together with extended life expectancy in most regions, is resulting in significant demographic differences between regions and corresponding variations in labour supply. This has resulted in varying attitudes towards migration and this volume reflects these variations through studies that are based in India and Eurasia. Certain commonalities are immediately evident, both in terms of the identification of the problem and in terms of solutions. Yet, each case is also specific to the region in which it is situated. This volume looks towards generating a debate that takes notes of both the commonalities and differences with a view to benefitting from these diverse experiences.

1

New Tendencies in East Asian Geopolitics

B.V. Bazarov and *N.I. Atanov*

The article is an analysis of the ongoing process of economic regionalism in East Asia. The various projects undertaken here display tendencies of a new form of Chinese regionalism called "global regionalism"[1] with visible signs of the economic rise of China in the course of which the growing demand for raw materials will be satisfied with the help of its neighbours. Chinese global regionalism that provides new positioning of China in the global arena is, in essence, a new Chinese global strategy. In this context the participation of China in the development of natural resources of East Siberia and the Far East, energy cooperation and cooperation in other spheres are important prerequisites of stable development of the Chinese economy.

The bilateral economic cooperation seems to be efficient and mutually beneficial only if there is a balance of domestic and foreign, short-term and long-term interests and perspectives of both parties. There is overall dependence of China on Russia as a stable source of raw materials, such as oil, gas, timber, non-ferrous and ferrous metals.

Technically, both sides are involved in joint development of mineral deposits in Russia and final production of goods in China. A large number of projects in timber industry along the entire perimeter of South-East Siberia and the Far East are, most probably, designed for dismantling and relocation of the old Chinese timber processing facilities to the Russian territory and installation of final woodworking production facilities in China (see attachment 1). There are also projects to build residential quarters and industrial zones. The final purpose of such construction remains unclear: whether it is for the outgoing Russian population of Siberia and the Far East or for the incoming Chinese settlers. The latter factor however, is not to be excluded because the same programme presupposes expansion and technical modernization of border crossing points as well as "strengthening of the Russo-Chinese cooperation in the labour sphere."

China is ready to build processing facilities on the Russian territory if they are operated by Chinese workforce. All this denotes a course towards primitive exploitation, but not hi-tech and innovative development of the Far East and Eastern Siberia. Certain doubts are also caused by bottling drinking water projects at Lake Baikal and in Kamchatka as if Russia lacked its own facilities and technologies for it.

The analysis of projects on the Chinese side shows stark differences from the Russian raw-material-based investment projects. China intercepts chemical and silicon projects of the Russian side as well as metal processing projects, hi-tech production of construction materials, mechanical engineering, light industry, etc. In what form the Russian investor will participate is yet unknown. And this is despite the fact that the joint Russo-Chinese Declaration clearly states that both parties will make efforts to create favourable conditions for the implementation of investment cooperation by the businesses of both countries, in order to set in motion the mechanisms of Russo-Chinese investment forums, increase the level and quality of mutual investments in both countries. Taking into account the weakness of Russia's investment resources the investment cooperation on the Chinese side will supposedly be one-sided.

There are many projects to develop the border crossing points, build and repair the border infrastructure. The main attention here is paid to the construction and quality improvement of roads, bridges, railroad crossing points, docking constructions, river crossings, etc. For example, the development of mineral deposits of the Zabaikalsii region requires reconstruction of the automobile crossing point Olochi – Shivei and construction of a railroad to the Mordaoga station from there. An agreement was also signed in the sphere of transport that encompasses all networks of ground, naval and air transportation (only in the Zabaikalskii region construction of three airports in Chita, Zabaikalsk and Krasnokamensk is planned). Again, transport infrastructure is clearly one-sided as far as the Chinese are concerned: from mineral deposits to border crossing points along the Russia-China border.

Energy security of China, that forms a separate point of the project, requires special consideration. China is ready to develop relations based on equality and mutual benefit. Energy sector is a sphere of cooperation where the interests of Russia, China and some other countries complement each other. Activation of the energy direction in the "global regionalization policy" of China is connected with new transnational challenges and threats, indirectly connected with problems of global leadership transformation and the existing world order.[2]

The modern level of trans-border interaction of the neighbouring regions does not correspond to its potential. Analyzing the contemporary state of trade and economic cooperation it is possible to come to a conclusion that at the moment it contributes to the solution of China's economic problems to a much greater extent than Russia's. Unequal exchange and a visible slowing down of the social and economic development of the frontier regions of Russia became a restraining factor in the development of the trade and economic relations between Russia and China. This requires special attention.

In this way, China pursues the following goals:

- to get access to East Siberian and Far Eastern deposits of mineral resources and pipelines, subjecting them to the domestic economic development problems of Northeast China;
- to purchase the most perspective assets in the spheres open for foreign investment capital;
- to secure leading positions of large Chinese companies in the regional economies of Siberia and the Far East compared with Russian and third party competitors;
- to make a diffusion on the eastern Russian region relative to other global competitors;
- to turn northern and northeastern provinces of China into a highly developed, rich and attractive border oasis;

According to our information, the PRC developed a plan of "cutting in" the Mongolian border along 8 roads. In an eastward direction, the roads are as follows:[3]

1. *The highway for large trucks planned for construction from the Chinese border crossing point of Takshken through the Mongolian border point Yarant situated in Buglan somon of the Khovd aimag, through Uench somon and to the city of Khovd.*
   This highway will be used for transporting coal from Khoshoot deposit. Prospectively, this road may be continued to the north of Mongolia to the administrative center of the Uvs *aimag* the city of Ulaangom and further on to Tyva Republic in Russia. In this way, there is a possibility to create a vertical highway in the western *aimags*. But the Chinese agree to build the road to the north only in one case if there will be a large mineral deposit. Most probably this planned road will be constructed by the engineering units of the Chinese army stationed in Sinkiang.
2. *The highway that is constructed through the border crossing point Burgastai of the Gov'-Altai aimag*
   This highway is built for transportation of iron ore from this *aimag* where the resources are practically twice as large as the Tomortei deposit in the Selenge *aimag*. Most probably this road will be also constructed by the PLA engineering units. It needs to be mentioned that 4 out of 7 military districts of the PLA are located along the Mongolian border. In the past the military strategy of China was based on the invasion of Mongolia and military action on the territory of our country in case the USSR attacked China. Consequently, the highway in this direction is closely connected with military strategy.

3. *The narrow-gauge railroad that the Chinese propose to build from the border point of Shiveekhuren, located in the western part of the South Gobi aimag, to Tavantolgoi deposit.*

   The minister of roads, transport and urban construction of Mongolia objects the construction of this railroad. He sincerely does not wish to open the "treasury doors" of Mongolia to the Chinese, saying, "If we open the border in two points in South Gobi all mineral wealth of Mongolia will flow out through them." Of course Mongolia needs this railroad. But one should remember that the Chinese railroad station of Tsekhe is situated in 80 km to the south from the border point of Shiveekhuren. Planning the construction of a railroad from this border point westwards, the Chinese will be able to connect it with their closest railway station.

   After building the narrow-gauge railroad in Mongolia the Chinese intend to continue it to the south until it reaches their railway station and then to transport coal through the underutilized western direction of their railroad. This is absolutely necessary because the railroad system of Northeast China is currently overburdened. Moreover, the western Chinese regions do not have large deposits of coal. China intends to use the Mongolian coal, especially thermal coal, for the development of their western region.

4. *The narrow-gauge railroad that is planned from Tavantolgoi to the border point of Gashuunsukhait.*

   This railroad will be constructed by "Energy Resource" consortium. Returning the Tavantolgoi development license this consortium managed to keep one of its parts, the 400 million ton "Ukhaa Khudag" deposit, in possession. "Energy Resource" intends to sell its coal to the Chinese and this is the main reason for construction of this railroad. To the south of the Mongolian border point Gashuun Sukhait there is a Chinese railroad station named Bayan-Ovoo. Within 100 km from this station there is a steelworks in the place called Bugat. The Chinese only recently finished construction of a railroad that connects Bugat with the railroad station at Bayan-Ovoo.

Unlike the route that passes through the border point at Shiveehuren, coal will be transported through this railroad. The construction of this railroad will allow the Chinese to transport coal from Tavantolgoi to the steelworks in Bugat through the shortest possible way. If to transport coal through Erlian, then a detour will be required first eastwards to the station of Zhinin, then 100 km further to Huh-hoto and then 100 more km to the steelworks at Bugat. If to measure the length of this route on a map till Bugat steelworks through Gashuun Sukhait, then this distance will be 4 times shorter than the distance from this steelworks through Erlian. Consequently, the direction through Gashuun Sukhait will allow saving considerably on transportation.

The Peoples' Republic of China occupies the third place in coal export in the world. At present the steelworks at Bugat functions on high-grade coal from a deposit in Shanxi province. According to its resources this deposit is practically comparable with the Mongolian Tavantolgoi. However, the trouble is that it is located in an elevated mountainous region and coal extraction is expensive. If the Chinese establish coal supply from Tavantolgoi, this will allow them to buy high-grade coal at a price twice lower than the international market price. For comparison we will remind that the price of Tavantolgoi coal will approximately be 50 USD and the price of coal imported from Australia will be higher than 100 USD. Supply of Mongolian coal for the Bugat steelworks will allow the Chinese using Shanxi coal for the well-known "Baosteel" steelworks located near Shanghai. Consequently, it is quite plausible to assume that the Tavantolgoi coal will end up in Bugat not reaching the port of Tianjin. The Chinese pay a lot of attention to the abovementioned railroads. If one takes into account the fact that Oyutolgoi and Tavantolgoi deposits are located practically in the center of the South Gobi aimag, one may say that the railroad directions through Gashuun Sukhait and Shiveehuren will form the "Golden Triangle" that will deeply cut into the Mongolian territory. It is easy to imagine the scale of profits that China will get through this triangle. In reality, coal extraction in China is relatively inexpensive. Perhaps this is why the railroad issue is regarded as the main factor of the Investment agreement on Tavantolgoi.

5. *The road that passes through Dzamyn-Erlian*

The Chinese side, especially the municipality of

Erlian is interested in the highway Choi-Dzamyn-Uud. Today a 12-km section of this highway south of Choir is not completed. In the direction of this road, which is a vertical axis, the Chinese already built a 14-km long highway from Erlian to Dzamyn-Uud. This direct highway connecting the Irkutsk region of Russia with Inner Mongolia has a profound strategic and economic significance. According to the Chinese gradation Erlian was earlier a grade 6 town, but now it has grown to the 4th grade. In other words, Erlian is at the same level as Huhhot. It is estimated that in the near future the population of Erlian will grow to 400,000 people and towards the end of the 11th Five-Year plan, to 1 million people. By making Erlian a special zone and creating a favorable tax climate, the Chinese government intends to attract investments from the southern regions of the country.

6. *The road through the border point of Bichigt*

   This road is for transporting ore from the zinc-iron deposit at Tomortei, which is located in Sukhe-Bator aimag. At present the Chinese support production with their domestic reserves because *Rio Tinto* and *BHP Billiton* stopped their supply of iron to China. This enterprise was built at the Tomortei deposit using a 300-million yuan loan from the Chairman of China as a token of appreciation for the fact that the Mongolians allowed the Chinese to develop the Tomortei ovoo deposit situated in the Selenga *aimag*.

7. *The road through the border point to Dornod aimag used for transporting crude oil*

Crude oil transported on this road is processed at the oil refinery at Huh-Hoto and the final products from this refinery are supplied back to Mongolia according to the Agreement to share produce. This amount makes up to 5 per cent of all Mongolian import of petrochemicals.

8. *The road passing through the border point Havirga*
   This road is also used for transporting crude oil. The reason why these two variants are so vigorously developed is in the drive of the Chinese to be ready for a variant according to which the Mongolians will build a full-gauge railroad in the direction of Choir-Choibalsan or Sainshand-Choibalsan.

In this way the Chinese got the opportunity for transportation of resources from all regions of Mongolia, starting from the town of Baitag in the west of the country to the eastern Mongolian-Russian borders.

The question "in what direction the railroad will be constructed" is the most important aspect of the investment agreement on Tavantolgoi. The Tavantolgoi project has greater prospects despite Russian economic restrictions and Chinese dumping policy. The investors have agreed to the strictures due to the availability of processed copper from Oyutolgoi deposit instead of copper ore. Similarly, the idea is to secure from a future partner in Tavantolgoi the supply of coal and electricity.

Thus, the emergence of new tendencies in the trans-border interaction of China with foreign neighbours is carried out in accordance with a rigid strategy. They depend on the peculiarities of a political setup and socio-economic development of neighbouring states. The solution of the issue became plausible and virtually insurmountable because the contemporary level of trans-border interaction of the frontier regions does not correspond to their potential. Analyzing the contemporary state of trade and economic cooperation, it is possible to come to a conclusion that today it contributes more to the solution of Chinese rather than Russian or Mongolian economic problems. The unequal exchange and slowing down of socio-economic development of frontier regions of Russia and Mongolia became the decisive factor of latent tendencies and the new strategy of China.

Notes and References

1. E.I. Safronova edited *Kitai v mirovoi i regional'noi politike: istoriya i sovremennost,* Moscow, 2008, p. 116.
2. Ya. Berger, 'Ob energeticheskoi strategii Kitaya', http://www.camegie.ru/ru/pubs/media/70487.htm Accessed on 20 February.
3. During the analysis of the "eight road strategy" the "Global Times" Chinese newspaper editor's article "Mongolia Keeps Biting On the Lower Lip" was used as well as an analytical report by Baatarkhuyag "The Iron Trap-2" from "Mongolia Today" on 13–14 January 2010.

2

Migration and its Consequences for Assam

With Special Reference to Illegal Immigration from Bangladesh

Homeswar Goswami

Migration is a form of geographical or spatial mobility between one spatial unit and another, generally involving a change of residence from the place of origin to the place of destination. Migration is a necessary element of normal population adjustment and equilibrium within a nation or a sub-national spatial unit. Unlike vital processes migration is rapid in its effects. It is closely connected with economic changes and with important national socio-economic and political events. Migration brings both quantitative and qualitative changes in the socio-economic and demographic characteristics of a region. Migration is now recognized as an important factor in determining plans for social, economic and political development, specially in developing countries. With a traditional social structure, a developing country which is going through a process of socio-economic transformation under conditions of political democracy, free migration of population has wider economic, political, social and cultural effects. The economist has been interested in the relation of migration to regional economic growth, business cycle, the supply of skill and unskilled labour, the growth of industry, outflow and inflow of money income, wage differences between the place of origin and place of destination of migrants, etc. The legislator and the political scientist are concerned with the formulation of policies and laws regarding immigration and to a lesser extent internal migration, and enfranchisement and voting behaviour of migrants. The sociologist is interested in the social, cultural and psychological effects of migration upon migrants as well as the general population in the place of destination or the process of assimilation and adjustment of migrant population. Some of the most acute social problems of the world today are associated with migration. If the problem of human fertility were not so critical at the present time, it is almost certain that human migration and the plight of migrants would be listed as the top priority problem for research and action.

The Role of Migration in Population Index

The importance of migration in effecting the growth and decline of population and in modifying the demographic characteristics of the areas of origin and areas of destination has long been recognized. The study of migration is one of the major branches of demography. In general, migration study is divided into two parts: internal migration and international migration. A migrant who crosses a migration defining boundary in the process of changing residence and enters a given community of some other part of the same nation is an internal migrant and is termed as 'in-migrant' while the term 'immigrant' refers to an international migrant who comes from a sovereign country. The area from which a migrant departs is termed as 'area of origin' and the area at which he arrives is termed as 'area of destination'. When a large number of migrants depart from a common area of origin and arrive at a common area of destination during a particular period of time, it is known as 'migration stream'.

There are a number of forces which act and react resulting in the movement of population from one place to another. In general, any action of human being is motivated by the desire to satisfy wants or to avoid discomforts or pain. Human organism tends to remain at rest until impelled to act by some unsatisfied wants or by the threat of discomforts. Migration research begins, therefore, with the premise that every departure for a new community is either a response to some impelling wants that the person believes that he cannot satisfy in his present residence or a flight from a situation that for some reason has become undesirable, unpleasant or intolerable. Thus certain 'push' and 'pull' forces are always in operation with the movement of population. A few examples of 'push' forces may be, decline in natural resources like mines, timber, or agricultural resources; loss of employment due to mechanization; oppressive or repressive discriminatory treatment because of political, religious or ethnic origin or membership; a retreat from a community because of catastrophic flood, fire, drought, earthquake or epidemic etc. Similarly, the 'pull' forces that may be in operation are better employment opportunities with larger income; preferable environment and living condition; opportunities to obtain the desired specialized education or training; desire for new or different activities, environment or people, such as attraction of cultural, intellectual or recreational activities of a metropolis.

Migration is an implantation of a new set of population into the indigenous population of the area of destination. Its consequences on the socio-economic and geo-political situation of the area of destination may be both positive and negative depending on the level of proximity of the migrants with the population of the area of destination in terms of ethnicity, religion, language, culture, social behaviour, economic pursuits, etc. in addition to the nature, quality, volume, composition, attitude, legal status etc. of the migrants. The purpose of this paper is to analyse the push and pull factors and the consequences of the major streams of migration that have taken place during pre and post-independence period in Assam, with special reference to illegal immigration from Bangladesh.

Migration during the Pre-Independence Period

With the annexation of Assam by the British, several streams of migrants originating from different parts of the sub-continent started entering Assam since the growth of British commercial interests in the mid nineteenth century. Five such prominent streams of migrants that have been identified are:

1. Tea garden labourers,
2. Muslim peasants from then East Bengal,
3. Bengali Hindus from East Pakistan (now Bangladesh),
4. Nepalese, and
5. Other migrants from different parts of India.

Tea Garden Labourers

The discovery of tea, its profitability and potentiality

encouraged British capitalists to cultivate Assam from the early decades of the 19th century. The acreage under tea and production thereof started growing rapidly from that time. But because of the scarcity of the local labourers the planters had to face serious difficulties in expanding tea cultivation C.A. Bruce, Superintendent of Tea Culture in Assam wrote in his report that 'the want of population, labourers and tea makers is acute. They will have to be imported and settled on the soil' (4). The Royal Commission on Labour in India, 1938 also spoke on similar lines. 'From the point of view of the employer, the outstanding problem during the whole history of tea plantating in Assam has been the scarcity of labour'. The Assam Labour Enquiry Committee of 1906 calculated that the Assam Valley labour force was short by about fifty thousand and the annual intake was about three thousand less than what was required; both calculations being made on the assumptions that for every garden and every acre, one and half labourers were required. The planters complained to Lord Curzon, the then Viceroy and Governor-General of India that 'scarcity of labour is one of the most serious and real difficulties with which we had to contend. The indigenous population has been wholly insufficient to develop the province'.

Such charges against the Assamese were unfounded. The reasons for not getting local labour lay elsewhere. About half of Assam Valley's population was lost during civil wars in the last quarter of the 18th century and the Burmese incursions in the first quarter of the 19th century. So, when the British occupied Assam Valley in 1826, many deserted villages were seen in the upper part of the Valley where tea gardens flourished later on. 'Large tracts, once inhabited by happy and numerous population, had been converted into extensive and unwholesome jungles'. The large scale depopulation and extensive vegetative growth had greatly changed the climatic condition of the Valley making it unhealthy, damp and enervating. The area became a hotbed of germs causing cholera, malaria, smallpox, dysentery, *kalaazar* and other tropical diseases which resulted in heavy tolls every year.

Secondly, the bulk of tea gardens were established in the uncultivated and mostly uninhabited belt of the valley. So the plantation need not require the displacement of any local cultivator who might have worked as labourers in the garden. The local cultivators were self-sufficient and hardly in need of cash except for the payment of land revenue which was nominal.

Thirdly, during slack agricultural seasons, the Assamese cultivators liked to use their leisure time in attending social and religious functions, visiting distant relatives and friends.

Fourthly, the settled agricultural people of Assam were averse to seek employment in the gardens as tea garden work was meant for unskilled people.

Fifthly, the local people were reluctant to work as garden labourers because the treatment meted out to them by the management which was extremely discouraging for the local peasantry.

The garden managements made several attempts to attract local people to work in the garden as labourers but without any success. A few gardens including the famous Assam Company in 1839–40 procured several batches of Chinese artisans and labourers on contract to work in their gardens. But the recruitment of Chinese tea makers was a costly affair. Moreover, the Chinese labourers were often quarrelsome.

The tea industry, therefore, ever since its establishment in Assam, had to import labourers from those parts of India where the population was denser, less secure, and more accustomed to working for wages. A Tea Planters Association was formed in 1886 for the purpose, inter-alias, of organizing a system of labour importation from Bengal, Bihar, Orissa, Chotanagpur, Central Provinces, United Provinces, Madras, Bombay to Assam Valley. Most of the labourers were brought along with other members of their family.

The principal recruiting areas of garden labourers generated several push factors which was the main motive force behind such migration. The exploitative system of land tenure and revenue assessment owing to permanent and temporary zamindari settlement created large army of landless labour class in the recruiting provinces. Moreover, severe famines and scarcities appeared frequently in the second half of the nineteenth century in these provinces. Thus, the demand for labour to work in the tea gardens of Assam generated a pull effect, the unfavourable economic conditions in the recruiting regions created a push effect to migrate.

The Muslim Peasants

The second batch of migrants was the Muslim peasants from East Bengal districts of Mymansingh, Pabna, Bogra and Rangpur. This immigration trend began as a result of the interplay of economic forces in East Bengal vis-à-vis the Assam valley. Though there was scarcity of land, famines and pestilence and long-standing congestion of population in East Bengal, people never migrated from there prior to the 20th century. The 1891 Census categorically stated that no cultivators from overcrowded Bengal did come to Assam. But economic and agrarian conditions gradually became unbearable for the depressed and landless labour class from the beginning of the 20th century. The extra ordinary rise in the prices of food grains, acute indebtedness, pressure of population on land, oppression of the *zamindars*, high land-rent etc. had created a strong desire in the minds of the agricultural labourers and other depressed classes of Eastern Bengal to escape from such unbearable hardships. Migration and settlement on farm lands in Assam offered an easy escape.

There also took place great improvements in railway transport between Eastern Bengal and Assam in the first decade of the 20th century. Prior to this period, the only conveyance between Assam Valley and Eastern Bengal was navigable river transport provided by the river Brahmaputra. But in 1902 the Valley was connected by railways with Western Bengal through Eastern Bengal and in 1904 with Eastern Bengal through the Suruma Valley. These developments in railways greatly reduced the remoteness of Assam from the rest of British India which had increased the mobility of the Bengal peasantry and large number of farmers from the overcrowded districts of Eastern Bengal started pouring into the Assam Valley from the first decade of the 20th century.

Moreover, the political development in India during the 20's of the 20th century also helped to attract East Bengal peasants to settle in Assam. The Congress leaders of Assam withdrew their support to the British in forming a government under the Reforms Act, 1919, due to the call of non-cooperation movement by Mahatma Gandhi. A new government was however formed in 1921 with support of leaders of the then All Assam Mohammedan Association and the Tea Planters of Assam. This government gave an implicit support to the incoming migration stream in the name of 'grow more food' campaign during 1921–38 which tilted the religio-ethnic composition of the Valley' population.

It was expected that this flow of migration from East Bengal would stop after the partition of 1947, since East Bengal became a part of Pakistan. But even after the partition of the country, the immigrants from East Pakistan continued to pour in Assam taking advantage of the relatives and acquaintances settled in Assam and subsequently with the patronage of some political leaders of Assam. Further, the old immigrant Muslim landed gentry of Assam known as *Mutabbars* encouraged immigration of farm labourers belonging to the same religious group of the then East Pakistan to Assam with a view to obtaining cheap agricultural labourers for their farms. Even the Bangladesh Government has been indirectly supporting the emigration of Bangladeshi farmers to Assam/India as they deny the existence of any Bangladeshi immigrants in India.

The Assam agitation of early 1980's generated a fear psychosis in the minds of the illegal Muslim immigrants of being deported and therefore, in 1991 census these immigrants from Bangladesh (former East Pakistan) did not disclose their place of birth correctly. The Assam agitation and the seriousness shown by the subsequent governments in controlling infiltration of immigrants have restricted the flow of immigration during 1980s. But in subsequent years the flow of immigration from Bangladesh started with renewed vigour. The poor economic growth, unsettled political condition of Bangladesh triggered off large scale illegal emigration to its better-off neighbour, i.e., India.

The Bengali Hindu Migrants

The third section of migrants is the Bengali Hindus who were brought by the British for their offices and for working in other professions. It happened because of their early initiation to English education and the British-India administrative system. The movement of this stream was intensified along with the opening of new railway lines, post and telegraph offices, development of tea and petroleum industries in particular. The Bengali clerks, doctors and lawyers monopolised the British Government jobs and professions. However, the most conspicuous mass migration of this section took place at the time of Partition and immediately thereafter. The feeling of insecurity of life and property of the Hindus in then East Pakistan led the movement to this section of population to India and Assam being the adjacent State had to receive a larger number of Hindu displaced persons. The process was further intensified when the refugee rehabilitation schemes were implemented by the Government and when they were given physical and social shelter by their relatives and acquaintances. The migrants belonging to this category are mostly engaged in service and commercial activities and they are concentrated in urban areas, especially in the Brahmaputra Valley towns. With the emergence of Bangladesh, a fresh stream of Bengali Hindu migrants entered Assam and their exact number is not known.

Nepali Migrants

The fourth stream of migrants into Assam consists of Nepali immigrants and the process started with the British occupation in Assam. The recruitment of Nepalese into British army dates back to 1815 when they defeated Kazi Amar Singh Thapa and according to the fifth provision of the agreement, the British secured the right to recruit Nepalese into British army.

However, the Government of Nepal was unwilling to allow its men to serve the British army and therefore *Gorkhas* of the Indian army on leave in Nepal were also encouraged to smuggle out recruits from Nepal and were rewarded by the British. The Nepalese Government disliked the clandestine operations and took strong measures to discourage it. Instances were found that some of the *Gorkhas* serving in Indian army on their return home on leave in Nepal were even put to death and property of those serving the Indian army was confiscated. As a result the British Government encouraged migration of *Gorkhas* from Nepal with their families and established *Gorkha* settlements in certain parts of India including Assam. The British administration first brought the *Gorkhas* as soldiers and subsequently as watchmen, official peons etc. for their personal services. Many of them remained here after retirement and settled permanently in Assam. However, later on, the fresh Nepali migrants began to come on their own accord and started settling in different parts of Assam. Thus, their movement grew stronger when they came in large number during the last few decades to take up cultivation and livestock in the uncultivated and hill slopes. They went more or less unnoticed because they preferred to settle mainly in the forest areas near the foothills along the northern border of Assam and occupied large areas of the forest land. Many of them live in the outskirts of urban areas supplying milk and fuel to the urban dwellers. At present a major part of the business of milk and milk products are in the hands of these Nepali migrants. Besides, still a large number of Nepalese are employed as porters, *chowkidars* and office peon throughout the State following the same tradition initiated by the British administration.

The total Nepali population in Assam was only 21,347 in 1901 constituting nearly 0.65 per cent of the total population of Assam, which increased to 83,306 in 1931. During the post independence period there was sudden increase in the immigration of Nepalese into Assam. Their number increased to 1,01,338 in 1951 to 2,15,213 in 1961, to 3,49,116 in 1971 and further to 4,32,519 in 1991. In 1991 the Nepalese constitute nearly 1.93 per cent of the State's population. Twenty one per cent of the total Nepali population in Assam is living in Sonitpur district followed by 17.60 per cent in Tinsukia district in 1991. The immigration of Nepali migrants still continues as the citizens of Nepal do not require any passport to enter India, under the terms of the Indo-Nepal Friendship Treaty of 1950, the Tripartite Delhi Agreement of 1951 and the 1956 Revised Indo-Nepal agreement. Thus, free interchange and flow of both countries' nationals as well as their right to win property in either country is allowed unhindered and without restrictions.

Migrants from different Parts of India

The fifth stream of migrants comprises of those from other parts of India seeking economic opportunities in trading, construction works and white collar jobs, particularly from Orissa, Andhra Pradesh, Madhya Pradesh, Rajasthan, Bihar, Punjab, Uttar Pradesh, Tamil Nadu, Kerala and West Bengal. *Marwari* migrants from Rajasthan came to Assam in very small numbers in pre-British period, but their movement became significant with the establishment of British rule and subsequent development of tea industry and other commercial and industrial establishments. They acted as money changers, bankers and general agents to the managers of tea-gardens, especially in old Sibsagar and Lakhimpur districts, operated the mustard trade in Kamrup and Goalpara districts, sold hardware and other articles imported from other parts of India and became dealers in rice and grains throughout the State. Thus they were successful in monopolizing practically the whole of the trade and commerce in Assam by the turn of the nineteenth century. The 1891 Census reported only 4,877 migrants from Rajputana and their number has increased to 22,000 in 1961 and further to 70,000 in 1971. They are mostly concentrated in the urban and industrial centres and virtually the entire business and commercial transactions of the State at present can be said to be in their control.

The migration from the States of Bihar and Uttar Pradesh also started with the beginning of British rule in Assam. The migrants were absorbed as washer-men, barbers, sweepers, cobblers, load carriers, wage labourers in construction and their inflow increased with the extension of railway lines and steamer service which opened new avenues of employment in Assam. Their inflow was further intensified after independence when their services were in great demand as a result of industrialisation and urbanisation in the region. Thus their concentration is found in the urban and industrial areas of the State.

The in-migration of the people from other States of India is mostly a post-independence phenomenon. Among these, the Punjabi migrants are somewhat economically more significant as they are mostly engaged in commercial and industrial establishments of their own while most of the other migrants are either salary holders in some companies or public sector undertakings, as a contractor or a wage labourer in construction activities. Most of the internal migrants from other States of India are found in the urban areas of the State.

To sum up, most of the above migration streams into the State took place with the annexation of Assam by the British administration from the early part of the 19th century and the inflow of such migrants increased considerably by the turn of the 20th century.

Post-independence Trends–Illegal Migration from Bangladesh

In this section an attempt has been made to highlight a few major socio-economic and political consequences of Bangladeshi migration.

Economic Consequences

The contribution made by this stream of migrants towards agricultural development of Assam during the earlier phase cannot be denied as they extended the area under cultivation and reduced wasteland, increased agricultural production and introduced the cultivation of cash crops like jute, vegetables, tobacco, oilseeds, sugarcane including poultry farming, etc. Thus, immigration had led to the emergence of surplus workers in agricultural sector which affected the wage level in the State adversely. It was found that during 1956–57 to 1970–71, the per capita real income of the non-cultivating wage earners recorded a 12 per cent *decline* in Assam against the national average *increase* of 59 per cent. Therefore, any further increase in working force either by natural growth or by immigration, with existing level of technology in the agricultural sector in Assam, will lead to further overcrowding of the sector resulting in more poverty, increased socio-political problems and stagnation of the economy.

The settlement of Muslim immigrants in Assam at the initial stage increased state income, agricultural productivity, expanded area under multiple crops and also encouraged local cultivators to adopt improved agricultural practices. But subsequently the immigration had put tremendous pressure on land leading to declining output per agricultural worker, enhanced the problem of unemployment and disguised unemployment.

Social Consequences

Since the language spoken and religion followed by the immigrants were different from those of the majority of the indigenous population of Assam, the indigenous population initially did not like their entry into the state. Initially, the immigrants did not create any problem for the indigenous society as they were exclusively settled in immigrant localities along riverine tracts. With the increase in their number they often encroached upon the government reserves and wasteland of the indigenous farmers. This led to frequent frictions with the local farmers who petitioned to the Indian National Congress. Ultimately, the Government had to interfere by introducing line system, colonization scheme and tribal belt to keep away the immigrants from the occupation of land in the periphery of the local people. To allay the fear of the Assamese and to obtain a permanent footing in Assam, the Muslim immigrants started accepting Assamese language and culture. As a result, the number of Assamese speaking population increased from 2 million in 1931 to 5 million in 1951.

Another serious consequence of the immigration from Bangladesh and also from Nepal was the environmental degradation with the fall in forest coverage in Assam. Large areas of forest land were encroached upon by both these streams of immigrants for settlement and cultivation. The state experienced declining percentage of land area under forests. It was 39 per cent in 1951–52 that declined sharply to 28 per cent in 1965–66 and further to 26 per cent 1976–77 which was far below the National Forest Policy's requirements of 33 per cent. However, with the Supreme Court's order of banning deforestation and the Government's policy of afforestation the percentage of land area under forests in Assam has marginally improved to about 30 per cent now.

Another social consequence of immigration was change in the agrarian structure of the state. A class of petty landlords and money lenders emerged from among the immigrants. This class of people was popularly known as *Mutabbars* among the immigrants.

This immigration had led to the emergence of a landless class in Assam which was almost unknown in the past.

Political Consequences

In democracy numerical strength makes real difference. With the changing demographic pattern tilting towards equal numerical strength between the Hindus and the Muslims in many immigrant dominated areas of the State, the immigration issue which was essentially a socio-economic problem assumed a political character as the immigration issue had strengthened Muslim communal politics in the province. The germs of communalism entered into the body politics of India as a disruptive force since the introduction of diarchy, under the Reforms Act of 1919. Subsequently it came to forefront when the principle of separate electorates for election to the local bodies was adopted in 1923.

The Government of India Act of 1935 introduced provincial autonomy and abolished the diarchy. The General Elections under this Act was held throughout the country in February, 1937. Out of 108 seats in the Legislative Assembly of Assam, the Congress won 33 seats (26 out of 29 from the Brahmaputra and 7 out of 12 from Surma Valley) and the Muslims won 34. Though Congress had single majority, it could not form a ministry without the help of other parties. All the Muslim members of the Assembly were united and elected Syed Saadullah as their leader and a coalition was formed. Saadullah joined the Muslim League in October, 1937 and introduced several measures which intensified the flow of immigration from East Bengal into Assam. In 1940, Saadullah introduced Land Development Scheme which encouraged the immigrants to encroach upon the wasteland of Assam. Saadullah aimed to make Assam a Muslim majority State, and he recommended to the census of 1941 that the population of Assam be classified on the basis of community rather than on the basis of religion. As a result, a large number of tribal people who had earlier enrolled themselves as Hindus, Christians and Buddhists were now included under the category 'tribal'. This means that the Hindu tribals of Assam had been shown as non-Hindus in 1941 Census. The Land Development Scheme and the Census policy of Saadullah were subjected to severe public criticism all over the Province.

The millions of illegal immigrants, suffering constantly from the fear of being deported, offered a fertile field for the politicians to sow the seeds of communal politics in the post-independence period. A few middle class educated immigrants emerged as saviours and participated in state politics. This group of politicians was led by Maulana Bhasani who had migrated to Goalpara district in 1928. The All Assam Students Union (AASU) took up the foreign national deportation issue in its Sivsagar conference during 7–10 March, 1979, and petitioned the deportation of all illegal foreign nationals from Assam and protect the Assamese identity. This appeal did not have any response from the government side because the immigrants were electorally very significant for the ruling party.

The movement on the issue of deportation actually started from April, 1979 when the electoral roll for the by-election to the Lok Sabha in the Mangaldoi constituency was published consisting of the names of a large number of illegal immigrants as voters. To pursue the foreign nationals' deportation issue, a broad based coordination organization called All Assam Gana Sangram Parishad (AAGSP) was formed. Initially the movement was peaceful and secular but gradually it took communal and sectarian turn in different regions. This movement continued for six years and culminated with the signing of the Assam Accord between AASU, AAGSP and the Central Government on 15th August, 1985. On 12–14 October, 1985, a political party called *Asom Gana Parishad* (AGP) was formed with the movement's leaders and some other agitators whose mission was to win political power in the forthcoming election.

Thus, the most important consequence of the Assam agitation was the emergence of a regional party, i.e., the AGP which formed the ministry in Assam in 1985 by replacing the traditional Congress Party.

Another important and far reaching fallout of the Assam

agitation was that the people of Assam in general and the youths in particular lost faith in the central government regarding the protection of Assamese identity. A section of the agitators joined the United Liberation Front of Assam (ULFA), a secessionist insurgent group of Assam. The ULFA and the other insurgent groups of the North East India established their camps in the neighbouring countries like Myanmar, Bhutan and Bangladesh to carry out insurgent activities in the region. After being flashed out from Bhutan by the Bhutanese Government, they concentrated their camps in Bangladesh.

Conclusion

It is difficult, if not impossible, to deport even an illegal immigrant once he settles in the place of destination. However, further inflow of such immigrants can be stopped if serious efforts are made. To control infiltration, the following measures can be suggested.

1. Strengthen border security arrangements.
2. Enhance budgetary allocation for border security.
3. The present National Population Policy has to be drastically changed. Measures for controlling illegal immigration to India should also be included in the National Population Policy. The Government of India's population control schemes through birth control and family welfare are not enough. Illegal immigration has neutralized the positive effects of family welfare measures. Therefore, the issue of checking illegal immigration across the border should

be given top priority in India's Population Policy.

4. Though the Border Security Force (BSF) and the Border Police (BP) of Assam personnel are posted for the same purpose of checking infiltration, it is alleged that there is no coordination between the two sides. The basic amenities provided to the Border Police Force are to be improved for efficient patrolling of the border. The dilapidated condition of the watch posts and the patrol posts is to be improved.
5. Proposal for second line of defense skilled in handling modern weapons.
6. The entire length of Indo-Bangla border excluding the 61 km of marshy and riverine areas, is to be fenced to stop illegal immigration and infiltration of insurgents from across the Indo-Bangladesh border.

No amount of border security force, fencing, etc. can permanently stop the infiltration from Bangladesh. The ultimate solution lies in economic and political cooperation between Bangladesh and India. Stronger measures for confidence building need to be activated in which India needs to play a bigger role.

Notes and References

1. *Multi-lingual Demographic Dictionary*, English Section, United Nations, Department of Economics and Social Affairs, New York, 1958, p. 46.
2. R. Mehrotra, 'Inter-state Migration and Regional Income Inequalities in India', 1951–61, *Dibrugarh University Research Journal*, Vol. I, pp. 11–24, 1972.
3. Donald J. Bogue, *Principles of Demography*, New York, John Wiley & Sons Inc., 1969, p. 752.

4. A letter from A.H. Danforth of Gauhati Missionary, to AJM Mills, Judge of Sadar Court, Calcutta, while camping at Gauhati on 19th July, 1853, in AJM Mills Report on the Province of Assam, Government of Bengal, Calcutta, 1854, Appendix I-A, p. xxx.
5. C.A. Bruce, Report on the Manufacture of Tea and on the Extent and Produce of bmn Tea Plantation in Assam, Government of Bengal, Calcutta, 1838.
6. Report of the Royal Commission on Labour in India, 1931, Government Press, Bombay.
7. Report of the Assam Labour Enquiry Committee, 1906, Government of Eastern Bengal and Assam, Calcutta, 1906.
8. A.R. Dhekial Phukan, *op. cit.* p. xiv.
9. His Excellency Lord Curzon's reply to the Address of Welcome presented by the people of Assam at Gauhati on the 13th March, 1900, in Addresses etc. *op. cit.*, p. 29.
10. A Hand Book of Castes and Tribes Employed in Tea Estates in North Eastern India, Tea Districts Labour Association, North Eastern India, Calcutta, 1924. p. 1.
11. W.W. Hunter, *Statistical Account of Assam,* Trubner & Co. London, 1879, p. 134.
12. Assam Valley Reassessment Report, Government of Assam, Shillong, 1893, p. 14.
13. Margaret Reed, *Indian Peasants Uprooted*, Longman, Green & Co., London, 1931, pp. 131–32.
14. C.M. Elliott, 'Agriculture and Economic Development in Africa-Theory and Experience, 1880–1914', in E.L. Jones and S.J. Woolf (eds.), *Agrarian Change and Economic Development*, Mathun & Co. Ltd., London, 1969, p. 125.
15. H. Goswami, *Population Trend in the Brahmaputra Valley*, Mittal Publications, Delhi, 1985, pp. 91–92.
16. Selection from the Records of Government of Bengal, Vol. xxxvii, 1859, p. 71.
17. *Ibid.*
18. H.A. Antrobus, *A History of Assam Company, 1839–1953*, T & A Constable Ltd. Edinburgh, 1957, p. 343.
19. *Ibid.*
20. K. Davis, *The Population of India and Pakistan*, Princeton University Press, Princeton, 1951, p. 116.
21. Report of the Indian Famine Commission, 1880, Government of India, Delhi.

22. H. Goswami, *op. cit.* p. 96.
23. Government of Assam Annual Reports on Immigration in Assam for respective years.
24. Letters from the Government of Bengal to the Commissioner of Assam, Assam Secretariat, File No. 132/242, 1871.
25. J.K. Gogoi, *Migration and Economic Development in Assam 1951–71*, Doctoral Dissertation, Jawaharlal Nehru University, New Delhi, 1984, p. 66.
26. Census of Assam, 1891, Report on Assam, p. 67.
27. Report on the Land Revenue Administration of the Province of Eastern Bengal and Assam for the Revenue Year 1906–07, Government of Eastern Bengal and Assam, Dacca, 1907, pp. 1–2.
28. Amalendu Guha, *Planter Raj to Swaraj*, Indian Council of Historical Research, New Delhi, 1977, p. 206.
29. Census of India, 1961, Assam, General Report, p. 252.
30. A. Saikia, H. Goswami, A. Goswami, *Population Growth in Assam 1951–1991 with Focus on Migration*, Akansha Publishing House, New Delhi, 2003, p. 114.
31. Vidya Bir Singh Kansakar, *Emigration, Remittances and Rural Development,* Centre for Economic Development and Administration, Tribhuvan University, Kathmandu, 1982, p. 77.
32. *Census of India*, 1951, General Report, p. 255.
33. Amalendu Guha, *op. cit.*, p. 211.
34. M. Sujaud Doullah, *Immigration of East Bengal Farm Settlers and Agriculture Development of the Assam Valley, 1901–1947*, Institute of Objective Studies, New Delhi, 2003, p. 150.
35. Report on the Line System Committee, Shillong, 1938, p. 5.
36. A.C. Bhuyan and others, *Political History of Assam*, Vol. II, 1920–1939, Government of Assam, 1978, p. 313.
37. *Ibid.* p. 317.
38. *Ibid.* p. 334.
39. The first coalition ministry of Saadullah continued from 1st April, 1937 to 18th September, 1938. Congress coalition of Gopi Nath Bordoloi from 19th September, 1938 to 17th November, 1939. The second coalition ministry of Saadullah from 17th November, 1939 to 25th December, 1941. Governor's rule from 25th December, 1941 to 25th August, 1942. The third coalition ministry of Saadullah from 25th August, 1942 to 11th February, 1946. The Congress ministry of Bordoloi from 11th February 1946 to 14th August, 1947.

40. A.C. Bhuya and others ed *Political History of Assam*, Vol. III, 1940–1947, Government of Assam, Guwahati, 1980, p. 266.
41. Girin Phukan, *Bengali Immigrants and Regionalisation of Politics in Assam*, West Bengal Political Science Review, Vol. I, No-2, Jan-Dec, 1998. p. 153.
42. Aloke Banerjee, *Times of India*, 10th June, 2004.
43. *The Assam Tribune*, 30th July, 2004.
44. R. Dutta Choudhury, *The Assam Tribune*, 19th April, 2004.
45. The new project involves construction of 77.5 km roads and 71.50 km fencing at a cost of Rs. 167 crore in Assam, 204 km roads and 201 km fencing at a cost of Rs. 198 crore in Meghalaya, 1021 km fencing in West Bengal at Rs. 440 crore, 246.5 km roads and 400 km fencing at Rs. 254 crore in Mizoram and 269 km roads and 736 km fencing at Rs. 275 crore in Tripura. Source: *The Assam Tribune*, May 24, 2004.

3

Implications of Regional Migration for the East and North East of India

Jayanta Kumar Ray

This paper deals with voluntary migration of the Muslims from Bangladesh. The extent of forced migration of the Buddhists and Hindus from Bangladesh is beyond the purview of this paper. The paper focuses on the migration of members of the majority community in Bangladesh (i.e., Muslims) to east and northeast India. The territory designated as Bangladesh since 16 December 1971, was known as East Bengal during 1947–1956, and as East Pakistan during 1956–1971. Since this migration is almost entirely illegal and surreptitious, the author prefers to substitute the term 'infiltration' for 'migration', and labels it as a great danger to India, especially east and northeast India.

Some Indians, however, appear to be apologetic on this grave issue. They are worried that they may offend the notion of secularism if they tell the truth about this subject. Therefore, they tend to concoct arguments to underplay the phenomenon of infiltration. For example, they point out that migration is a worldwide phenomenon. But this observation is thoroughly misleading. For, the impact of migration in other parts of the world is far different from the impact of Bangladeshi Muslim infiltration upon eastern/north-eastern

India. For instance, the Mexican migrants to the United States, as also the Indian migrants to Britain, Canada or the United States do not disturb the demographic and electoral balance in the host country. Moreover, Mexico or India does not sponsor terrorism in the United States or elsewhere. In contrast, for many years, Pakistan has been named as the centre of worldwide terrorist operations. China also has an active role in this matter.

Undoubtedly, all infiltrators are not terrorists, and all terrorists are not infiltrators. Many of them are economic refugees. But, obviously, economically weak persons can be lured with monetary incentives, and can be recruited for terrorist activities. Moreover, at the very least, these poor infiltrators can provide sanctuaries to terrorists – irrespective of whether they are Bangladeshis, Pakistanis or Afghans.

Again, many politicians in India fall into the democracy trap when they try to deny the significance of infiltration. In 1981, for instance, *The Statesman* of Calcutta published a series of reports on the extent and impact of infiltration from Bangladesh to West Bengal. But the then Chief Minister of West Bengal castigated these reports as imaginary. Evidently, he was anxious to preserve his party's vote banks among infiltrators. In 1991, Hiteswar Saikia became the Chief Minister of Assam. He virtually ignored the growing menace of infiltration from Bangladesh to Assam, as he made no attempt to carry out his pledge, offered when he was yet to become the Chief Minister that he would drive out the Bangladeshi infiltrators from Assam.

Another way of deliberately underplaying the threat of infiltration is to deplore the lack of absolutely accurate figures about the number of infiltrators. In this context, one must remember that on many important socio-economic matters, it has not been possible to collect absolutely accurate statistics, e.g., on the exorbitantly high rate of interest charged by village moneylenders, the amount of black money in circulation in the country, or the quantity of smuggling between India and Bangladesh. Yet, on all these vital matters, approximately correct estimates are available, and they provide a reliable base for the formulation and implementation of public policies. This is also true of infiltration. A review of data in the census and election commission reports of Bangladesh and India indicate that at least 6.25 million Muslim infiltrators came from Bangladesh to India's eastern and north-eastern region during 1981–1991.

This is indeed a cause for worry. No less worrisome is the tendency of the Government of India to suppress data about infiltration. This may be the reason why the Indian census report of 1991 did not provide separate figures for Hindu and Muslim population, although it published such figures for Scheduled Castes and Scheduled Tribes. On 17 August 1995, P.M. Sayeed, the Union Minister of State for Home, while responding to a question by Rajnath Sonkar Shastri, a Congress Member of the Parliament, disclosed all the data about the relative population growth rates of different religious groups. The total population growth rate during 1981–91 stood at 36.83 per cent in Arunachal Pradesh (for instance), whereas the rate for Muslims stood at 135.01 per cent. The respective rates were 39.70 per cent and 105.80 per cent in Mizoram. Those who are bent upon underplaying infiltration may retort that Arunachal Pradesh and Mizoram are States with small population, and the total number of Muslim infiltrators may not be appreciably high. Let us then turn to a state with a large population, viz., West Bengal. Not to speak of border districts, even in the interior districts of West Bengal, e.g., Midnapore and Bankura, the disparity in the population growth rate for Hindus and Muslims in West Bengal during 1981–91 is disturbing: these rates are, for Hindus and Muslims respectively, 19.74 per cent and 53.80 per cent in Midnapore, and 14.33 per cent and 38.71 per cent in Bankura.

In order to comprehend the importance of infiltration, it may be useful to study the population growth rates in Bangladesh and West Bengal during 1981–91. The United Nations estimated this rate for Bangladesh at 2.7 per cent annually, the fertility rate being 4.5. But the actual rate turned out to be 2.1 per cent, which was totally inconsistent with the fertility rate. In contrast, in West Bengal, the actual decadal rate (24.55 per cent) was much higher than the estimated rate (20.7 per cent). This contrast could only be explained by massive infiltration from Bangladesh. This assessment could be reinforced by another fact: in the 1971–81 decade the population growth rate in West Bengal was 23.2 per cent – but for infiltration, in 1981–91, this rate should certainly have declined in a progressive state like West Bengal.

Another worrisome impact of infiltration upon West Bengal is the expulsion of Hindus from border districts. Since secularism forbids the utterance of plain truths, Union Minister of State for Home, P.M. Sayeed, hinted at this impact on 17 August 1995 in a euphemistic manner. He admitted that infiltration from Bangladesh was responsible for the growth of Muslim population in West Bengal and other border areas, and he confessed to: "locals are migrating into the interior" of West Bengal. By "locals" Sayced meant Hindus.

Whether before or after this significant date, 17 August 1995, authorities in New Delhi, Calcutta or Guwahati did not appear to be determined to curb infiltration. The so-called national media too largely refrained from taking up this vital issue. In September 1992, Debaprasad Roy, a Joint Secretary of All India Congress Committee, sent a note to the Union Home Minister, which, based on data collected from law-enforcing agencies, affirmed the presence of twenty million infiltrators in West Bengal. This note further asserted that in 132 Assembly constituencies of West Bengal, the number of voters increased by 40–50 per cent, whereas in another 34 constituencies this number rose by as much as 50–92 per cent.

In a report submitted to their party's High Command in 1993, Congress Party leaders of seven north-eastern States of India contended that Bangladeshi intelligence agencies, in collusion with their Pakistani counter parts, were trying to destabilize India's north-eastern region. Pakistan's ISI, this report stressed, was procuring funds from the Bank of Credit and Commerce International to carry out subversive activities in India. Pakistan, moreover, was training hundreds of officers of the Bangladesh army for cross-border operations. Congressmen referred to a Union Home Ministry study, which noted that infiltrators from Bangladesh had overturned the demographic and electoral balance of Assam by their overwhelming presence in sixteen of Assam's eighteen districts.

But authorities at Union and State levels failed to pay necessary attention to the interlinked problems of infiltration and terrorism. Prakash Singh, the Director General of India's Border Security Force, addressed an important letter to the Union Home Ministry just before his retirement on 31 January 1994. This letter warned that, unless requisite measures were taken to counteract infiltration and terrorism, a Kashmir-type situation might develop soon in the entire northeast of India. In late 1999, Lt. Gen. (Retd.) S.K. Sinha, the Governor of Assam, sent a 42-page report to the President of India. According to this report, infiltration was so large and ceaseless that it not only disrupted Assam's demographic balance but also obscured the identity of its people, and jeopardised India's national security. Sinha's report naturally focused on the role of Pakistan's ISI operating from Bangladesh to sustain terrorism in Assam. In early 1999 and on many occasions subsequently, Manik Sarkar, the Chief Minister of India's Tripura State, declared publicly that there were a large number of camps in Bangladesh, which provided operational bases for terrorists in northeast India.

In 1999, nearly eighteen years after the Chief Minister of West Bengal refused to recognize the problem of infiltration, the West Bengal government acknowledged the realities in an affidavit before the Supreme Court. This affidavit, submitted in connection with public interest litigation on infiltration, stated unambiguously that local touts, as also a section of politicians and government officials, obviously to build and sustain vote banks, provided extensive patronage to infiltrators. Thus, infiltrators could possess ration cards or manipulate entry into the voters' lists. By this point of time, remarkably, ISI hideaways emerged in a large number of *madrasas* and mosques situated in various parts of West Bengal (including Kolkata). West Bengal police had to raid these places, where terrorists connected with serial explosions in Mumbai and New Delhi had taken shelter. As before, the national media remained grossly negligent in alerting the public to such alarming developments.

On 20 April 2000, General (Retd.) Shankar Roy Chowdhury, a former Chief of the Indian Army, made a statement at the Rajya Sabha. Like P.M. Sayeed on 17 August 1995, Roy Chowdhury employed a lot of euphemisms to depict the impact of infiltration upon West Bengal. Despite euphemisms, attesting to a deeply ingrained sense of secularism, Roy Chowdhury's message could not be missed: Muslim infiltrators converted a 10–20 km belt in West Bengal's border zone into an informal extension of the political boundary of Bangladesh. What Roy Chowdhury did not clearly convey, but what has been brought out in unofficial investigations by researchers, is that over the years a number of Hindu-majority villages in the border zone of West Bengal have been converted into Muslim-majority villages, whereas Muslim-majority villages have gradually witnessed the total disappearance of the Hindu population.

All these threats to security have not provoked adequate countermeasures by India. Bangladesh has merrily provided sanctuaries to leaders of rebel outfits in northeast India. In collaboration with Pakistan, it has also provided training facilities to these outfits. Protests by India have not yielded any visible result. In the forests of Bhutan too these outfits built sanctuaries and training camps. Eventually, in the early part of 2004, authorities in Bhutan destroyed these sanctuaries by military action, not because India requested them to do so, but because the activities of militants so expanded as to threaten Bhutan's security.

There is an allegation that behind this failure on the part of India lies the determination of the Indian decision makers that nothing should be done to disturb trade between India and Bangladesh. The National Council of Applied Economic Research (NCAER), New Delhi, published in 1995 an elaborate study of smuggling across the West Bengal-Bangladesh border. This report noted what can be confirmed by direct observation at the border – that essential articles of everyday use (e.g., livestock, vegetable oil, spices, cycles, fabrics and yarns, parts of a wide variety of machines, etc.) are smuggled from India to Bangladesh in huge quantities. The NCAER study has rightly identified – and this too can be corroborated by direct observation at the border – the glaring absence of a comparable flow of essential commodities from Bangladesh to India by way of smuggling. The mystery how, then, smugglers on both sides of the border settle their accounts can be resolved by reference to gold, narcotics and arms being smuggled from Bangladesh to India, and providing sustenance to terrorists in northeast India. In this way, Indian authorities, unable to combat such smuggling, become a party to the perpetuation of terrorism in northeast India.

It is advisable to be more specific on how infiltration poses a threat to the socio-economic-political stability of West Bengal, a key state in eastern India. In every district of the state during 1951–2001, there has been a decline in Hindu population, and an extraordinary upswing in Muslim population. In a number of districts, the rate of growth of the Muslim population has been double or more than double that of the Hindu population. During 1951–2001, growth rates of Hindus and Muslims have been, respectively, 198.54 per cent and 310.93 per cent. In 1951, population share of Hindus and Muslims was, respectively 78.45 per cent and 19.85 per cent. In course of the next fifty years, by 2001, the share of Hindus in Bengal dwindled to 72.47 per cent (a decrease by 6%), whereas the share of Muslims rose to 25.25 per cent (an increase of 5.40%).

In the perspective of the Partition of British India in 1947 on the basis of religion, and the unfortunate (though unavoidable and hypocritically unacknowledged) perpetuation of communal antagonism as a result of Partition, one aspect of growth of population as per the India Census of 2001 deserves special attention. In the age group of 0–6 years, the growth rate of Hindus and Muslims stands at, respectively, 12.69 per cent and 18.7 per cent. Among all religious groups in West Bengal, the share of Muslims in the 0–6 age group stands at 33.17 per cent, although the population share of Muslims in the State, as already stated, is only 25.25 per cent. In contrast, the share of Hindus in the 0–6 age group is only 64.61 per cent, in spite of their population share of 72.47 per cent. This excessive increase of Muslims in the 0–6 age group points to an ominous consequence. Even if one assumes (although this is an absurd assumption) that there will be no infiltration in West Bengal till 2040, Muslims will form a majority in West Bengal by 2040. If infiltration continues, this demographic change will take place much earlier – not later than 2035. Even a person of purest liberal conscience cannot view this with equanimity. For, it is the lesson of world history that (barring insignificant exceptions) whenever Muslims become a majority in a territory, they try to form an independent political entity, and resort to ethnic expulsion.

4

Migration in Post-Soviet Central Asia: Problems and Perspectives

Gulnara Mendikulova

Migration in Central Asia

In the historical past, migration influenced the changing of ethnic composition, political, economical and cultural situation, development in the Central Asian region, as well as elsewhere in the World[1] (See Table 1). In 1990s after the break down of the "Iron Curtain" and the collapse of the USSR, borders were opened[2] and new conditions for migratory processes in Eurasia have been created. In the Central Asian region intensification of migratory movements were increased by large-spreading external and internal geopolitical and economical causes, interethnic and war conflicts.

In early 1990s, there were a few external and internal, voluntary and forced migratory waves in Central Asia, such as:

- emigration,
- repatriation or return migration,
- all types of refugee movements,
- brain-drain,

Table 1: Population, Health, and Environmental Data and Estimates for the Countries and Regions of the World[1]

	Population mid-2009 (millions)	Births per 1,000	Population Deaths per 1,000	Population Rate of Natural Increase (%)	Net Migration Rate per 1,000	Projected Population (millions) mid–2025	Projected Population (millions) mid–2050	Projected Population Change 2009–2050 (%)	Infant Mortality Rates	Total Fertility Rates	Percent of Population Ages <15	Percent of Population Ages 65+
South Central Asia	1,726	24	7	1.7	-0	2,148	2,624	52	57	2.8	32	5
Afghanistan	28.4	39	18	2.1	6	39.4	53.4	88	155	5.7	44	2
Bangladesh	162.2	23	7	1.6	-1	195.0	222.5	37	48	2.5	32	4
Bhutan	0.7	25	8	1.7	3	0.9	1.0	46	40	3.1	32	5
India	1,171.0	23	7	1.6	-0	1,444.5	1,748.0	49	55	2.7	32	5
Iran	73.2	20	5	1.5	-1	88.0	100.2	37	35	2.0	28	5
Kazakhstan	15.9	23	10	1.3	0	18.0	21.1	33	32	2.7	24	8
Kyrgyzstan	5.3	24	7	1.6	-10	6.5	8.0	52	31	2.8	30	5
Maldives	0.3	22	4	1.8	0	0.4	0.5	51	10	2.3	30	5
Nepal	27.5	29	9	2.1	-1	35.7	46.0	67	48	3.1	37	4
Pakistan	180.8	30	7	2.3	-2	246.3	335.2	85	67	4.0	38	4
Sri Lanka	20.5	19	7	1.2	-2	23.2	25.4	24	15	2.4	26	7
Tajikistan	7.5	28	5	2.3	-2	10.2	13.7	84	65	3.4	38	4
Turkmenistan	5.1	22	8	1.4	-1	6.1	6.8	33	51	2.5	31	4
Uzbekistan	27.6	23	5	1.8	-2	34.4	42.4	54	48	2.6	33	5

1. Population Reference Bureau. *2009 World Population Data Sheet*. Washington, D.C.: Population Reference Bureau, 2009. p. 8.

- labour migration,
- trade and business migration,
- mixed (polyethnic) marriage,
- traffic and illegal migrations,
- other (irregular, season, and etc.).

All these types of migrations are influenced integration of the Region[3]. It may be noted that forced migrations are the main part of these trends.

Migrations of the 2000s in the Region are different from the 1990s and displays the following features:

- labour migration,
- repatriation or return migration,
- trade and business migration,
- all types of traffic,
- illegal migrations,
- transit corridor; and etc.[4]

Now a few words about these migratory trends in Central Asia.

Emigration of Repatriation from Central Asia

At the beginning of 1990s repatriation was the typical phenomenon in migratory trends from Central Asia, as well as from territory of all former Soviet Union. It is estimated that in the first years of independence, almost 2 million people left Kazakhstan in search of a different life, including more than a million ethnic Russians and other Slavs, as well as almost 600,000 ethnic Germans, 50,000 Greeks and others.

As for Central Asia about 4,5 million people left the Region up to now[5]. (See Tables 2-5).

Repatriation

Return Migration to Central Asia

Integration into a new society is always difficult in social-economical, psychological and cultural spheres. It may be even more difficult in the western countries with different mentality, untraditional cultural environment that is why we have return migration (or re-emigration) to Central Asia by the same emigrants. Since 1989 until 2007 more than 300 thousand re-emigrants from Germany, Russia, Ukraine and other countries has returned to Kazakhstan[6].

Table 2: Some Data on Immigration to Kazakhstan for Permanent Residence, 1989-1999, by Oblasts

From *To Oblasts*	*Kyrgyzstan*	*Russia*	*Tajikistan*	*Uzbekistan*	*Afghanistan*	*China*	*Mongolia*	*Turkey*	*Iran*
Akmola	**1051**	**8192**	**301**	**937**	**1**	**4**	**8508**	**13**	**–**
Including Kazakhs	33	1800	9	399	–	–	8453	–	–
Aktobe	**129**	**3721**	**47**	**852**	**9**	**3**	**982**	**8**	**24**
Kazakhs	17	2034	11	644	5	1	982	1	24
Almaty	**2357**	**7873**	**793**	**18639**	**253**	**565**	**7295**	**539**	**198**
Kazakhs	390	1625	94	15535	248	506	7181	468	193
Atyrau	**26**	**714**	**30**	**243**	**–**	**1**	**–**	**24**	**–**
Kazakhs	3	381	4	134		1			
Eastern–Kazakhstan	**829**	**13678**	**339**	**899**	**8**	**168**	**4198**	**48**	**–**
Kazakhs	90	1311	28	139	–	151	4054	7	–
Jambyl									
Kazakhs	1224	481	581	11149	76	139	43	9	79
Western–Kazakhstan	**138**	**4467**	**95**	**372**	**–**	**1**	**4**	**2**	**–**
Kazakhs	13	2344	7	101		1	2	–	
Karaganda	**971**	**8565**	**621**	**2002**	**–**	**47**	**10247**	**67**	**1**
Kazakhs	105	696	47	1325		28	10122	3	–
Kostanai	**476**	**15045**	**300**	**646**	**2**	**5**	**1248**	**13**	**–**
Kazakhs	19	2985	14	107	–	–	1208	1	

From To Oblasts	Kyrgyzstan	Russia	Tajikistan	Uzbekistan	Afghanistan	China	Mongolia	Turkey	Iran
Kyzylorda	**69**	**215**	**113**	**747**	**27**	**3**	**7**	**9**	**6**
Kazakhs	37	67	69	614	27	2	7	4	6
Mangystau	**206**	**5123**	**166**	**6652**	**21**	**3**	**–**	**45**	**780**
Kazakhs	21	1445	82	6341	21	3		41	766
Pavlodar	**695**	**11075**	**214**	**513**	**–**	**94**	**6898**	**36**	**1**
Kazakhs	24	3404	25	71		94	6898	7	–
Northern–Kazakhstan	**663**	**9120**	**304**	**499**	**2**	**4**	**2722**	**27**	**–**
Kazakhs	16	2425	9	100	–	–	2712	1	
Southern–Kazakhstan	**456**	**2446**	**4927**	**16934**	**672**	**49**	**26**	**534**	**1790**
Kazakhs	101	437	4357	13605	632	14	23	372	1784
Astana city	**187**	**2119**	**16**	**311**	**–**	**88**	**374**	**67**	**–**
Kazakhs	47	506	5	126		6	364	4	
Almaty city	**1960**	**9510**	**860**	**4682**	**189**	**831**	**496**	**275**	**89**
Kazakhs	455	2539	134	3148	20	506	457	58	23

Source: Agency on Statistics of the Republic of Kazakhstan, *Results of the 1999 Census of Population of the Republic of Kazakhstan. Statistical Handbook,* Almaty: Agency on Statistics of the Republic of Kazakhstan, 2000, pp. 86–129.

Table 3: External Migration in Kazakhstan (except ethnic Kazakhs), 2000-2002

(*persons*)

	2000			2001			2002		
	Immigrants	*Emigrants*	*+/-*	*Immigrants*	*Emigrants*	*+/-*	*Immigrants*	*Emigrants*	*+/-*
Total	47442	155749	- 308307	53548	141710	- 88162	58162	120150	- 61988
Kyrgyzstan	1673	736	937	2145	548	1597	2564	584	1980
Russia	23941	108724	-84783	23497	94917	- 71420	21741	80001	- 58260
Tajikistan	617	76	541	464	47	417	380	38	342
Turkmenistan	2058	85	1973	2947	50	2897	3174	59	3115
Uzbekistan	12810	1277	11533	18783	1032	17751	24602	960	23642
Mongolia	658	207	451	407	126	281	476	23	453
Turkey	919	28	891	385	52	333	170	59	111

Source: Agency on Statistics of the Republic of Kazakhstan, *Kazakhstan in Figures,* Astana: Agency on Statistics of the Republic of Kazakhstan, 2003, pp. 31–32.

Table 4: External Migration in Kazakhstan (except ethnic Kazakhs), 2003-2004

(persons)

	2003			2004		
	Immigrants	*Emigrants*	*+/-*	*Immigrants*	*Emigrants*	*+/-*
Total:	65584	73890	-8306	68319	65530	2789
CIS countries	60781	49260	11521	61831	46929	14902
Kyrgyzstan	2818	461	2357	2612	304	2308
Russia	21565	45451	-23886	18565	44215	-25650
Tajikistan	316	31	285	261	53	208
Turkmenistan	3336	39	3297	3266	31	3225
Uzbekistan	31191	982	30209	35795	678	35117
Not from CIS countries	4803	24630	-19827	6488	18601	-12113
Germany	776	22520	-21744	764	17221	-16457
Israel	94	328	-234	91	248	-157
Canada	31	398	-367	31	309	-278
Mongolia	1177	43	1134	1607	50	1557
turkey	239	51	188	129	35	94
USA	46	422	-376	38	335	-297
Lithuania	6	20	-14			
Estonia	-	2	-2			

Source: Agency on Statistics of the Republic of Kazakhstan, *Statistical Yearbook of Kazakhstan,* Astana: Agency on Statistics of the Republic of Kazakhstan, 2007, pp. 26–28.

Table 5: External Migration in Kazakhstan (except ethnic Kazakhs), 2005-2006

(*persons*)

	2005			2006		
	Immigrants	*Emigrants*	*+/-*	*Immigrants*	*Emigrants*	*+/-*
Total:	74807	52139	22668	66731	33690	33014
CIS countries	65829	40698	25131	56635	30271	26364
Kyrgyzstan	2596	168	2428	2397	130	2267
Russia	15022	38498	-23476	15001	28228	-13227
Tajikistan	197	58	139	684	38	646
Turkmenistan	2397	21	2376	4565	17	4548
Uzbekistan	44648	619	44029	32620	608	32012
Not from CIS countries	8978	11441	-2463	10096	3419	6677
Germany	675	10299	-9624	615	2528	-1913
Israel	48	118	-70	81	123	-42
Canada	24	285	-261	38	182	-144
Mongolia	3104	38	3066	3648	43	3605
turkey	287	17	270	343	6	337
USA	39	294	-255	37	235	-198
Lithuania						
Estonia						

Source: Agency on Statistics of the Republic of Kazakhstan, *Statistical Yearbook of Kazakhstan,* Astana: Agency on Statistics of the Republic of Kazakhstan, 2007, pp. 26–28.

Repatriation to Kazakhstan

At the same time, repatriation of ethnic Kazakhs from different countries took place since 1992. The process of repatriation of ethnic Kazakhs may be divided into two stages, such as: since 1992 until 1997, when the Law about Migration was passed[7]; and since 1997 until now when all *Oralmans* could come to Kazakhstan by quotas, according to those the essential conditions for living, working and education were granted to[8].

In Kazakhstan, the beginning of the repatriation's process was connected with refugee problems, because a part of the Kazakh people, especially in Iran, required state protection. The Kazakh minority in Iran is descendants of those who fled from the Soviet State during the Civil war (1918–1920) and Collectivization (1929–1932). Some of them are Kazakh war refugees from Afghanistan in 1980s. These Afghani Kazakhs were war refugees, but until 1993 they did not obtain citizenship or any support from the Iranian government. They lived in Iran in very poor living conditions for more the one-decade without housing and proper documents.

Therefore, Kazakhstan began negotiations with Iran about the process and procedure of repatriation of these Kazakhs. In February 1993, the Agreement between Kazakhstan and Iran about the repatriation of the Kazakh refugees was signed, giving an opportunity for a few thousand of the Kazakhs to go to Kazakhstan.

Furthermore, after those events the Immigration law (1996) was passed, according to which every ethnic Kazakh immigrant was granted refugee status. Among them were 4,000 refugees from Tajikistan, 11,000 from Afghanistan and

Table 6: Number of Oralmans Came to Kazakhstan per Oblast. 1991-1st October 2008

No.	Oblasts	*Total*		*Including*			
		Families	*Persons*	*Men*	*%*	*Women*	*%*
1	Akmola	7451	38233	17674	46.2	20559	53.8
2	Aktyube	6819	33759	15584	46.2	18175	53.8
3	Almata	30049	102023	49749	48.8	52274	51.2
4	Atyrau	3656	14998	7250	48.3	7748	51.7
5	Eastern-Kazakhstan	8945	35069	15925	45.4	19144	54.6
6	Jambyl	11123	63983	31351	49.0	32632	51.0
7	Western-Kazakhstan	3172	14234	6902	48.5	7332	51.5
8	Karaganda	12998	46273	22311	48.2	23962	51.8
9	Kostanai	5891	24573	11795	48.0	12778	52.0
10	Kyzylorda	3542	17314	7943	45.9	9371	54.1
11	Mangystau	24460	85464	34727	40.6	50737	59.4
12	Pavlodar	6175	28072	13064	46.5	15008	53.5
13	Northern-Kazakhstan	6439	33951	14752	43.5	19199	56.5
14	Southern-Kazakhstan	45827	155963	73438	47.1	82525	52.9
15	Almaty city	1778	6471	3162	48.9	3309	51.1
16	Astana city	1199	5661	2632	46.5	3029	53.5
	All	179524	706041	328259	46.5	377782	53.5

Source: Agency on Statistics of the Republic of Kazakhstan, *Cóllected Data 1991, 1st October 2008; Kazakh Eli.* 24th Nauryz 2009, pp. 5–6.

Table 7: Number of the Kazakhs Came from China to Kazakhstan for Permanent Residence, 1989–1998 (by ages)

	Both Genders	*Men*	*Women*	*Urban Population*			*Rural Population*		
				Both Genders	*Men*	*Women*	*Both Genders*	*Men*	*Women*
Total:	2026	1130	896	1253	724	529	773	406	367
By ages:									
0–4 ages	25	11	14	17	7	10	8	4	4
5–9	126	69	57	72	40	32	54	29	25
10–14	169	74	95	67	29	38	102	45	57
15–19	159	77	82	82	38	44	77	39	38
20–24	167	107	60	115	75	40	52	32	20
25–29	184	117	67	128	88	40	56	29	27
30–34	204	110	94	160	86	74	44	24	20
35–39	238	141	97	161	106	55	77	35	42
40–44	233	146	87	145	96	49	88	50	38
45–49	170	95	75	109	61	48	61	34	27
50–54	93	55	38	65	33	32	28	22	6
55–59	88	44	44	51	25	26	37	19	18
60–64	78	40	38	40	20	20	38	20	18
65–69	44	22	22	21	12	9	23	10	13
Elder then 70	48	22	26	20	8	12	28	14	19

Source: Agency on Statistics of the Republic of Kazakhstan, *Results of the 1999 Census of Population of the Republic of Kazakhstan. Statistical Handbook,* Almaty: Agency on Statistics of the Republic of Kazakhstan 2000.

Iran, 90,000 from Mongolia, 2,000 from Turkey, 390 thousand from CIS countries (especially, from Russia and Uzbekistan), and 2000 from China[9]. In 1997 the Law on Migration was passed, according to which every ethnic Kazakh immigrant was granted the status of *oralman.* The Government of Kazakhstan established Migration Department within the Ministry of Labour and Social Protection, which now is called as Agency of Migration and Demographic Policy. Since 1993 until early 2010 more than 700 thousands Oralmans (Kazakh ethnic repatriates) moved to their historical Homeland[10].

All Types of Refugee Movements

Armed Conflict or War Refugees

Following the collapse of the USSR and the declaration of independent Kazakhstan, the repatriation and refugee problem became even more acute. A number of inter-ethnic and political conflicts were taking place in Central Asia. As a result, several waves of refugees entered Kazakhstan from Tajikistan (since 1992), Chechnya (since 1995) and other places. These refugees can be economically categorized as poor. A longer and more wide-ranging conflict was the civil war, which erupted in Tajikistan in 1992. At least 20,000 people were killed and over 1 million displaced. 600 thousand people were displaced within the country while another 250,000 fled to Afghanistan and neighbouring Central Asian states, particularly, to Kazakhstan[11]. By late 1995, over two-thirds of the refugees in Afghanistan returned home, but Tajik refugees are still found in the Central Asian republics. In 1990s fear of actual or real violence, as well as extreme economic hardship and instability, prompted many of

Tajikistan's refugees to return home. Now the situation is changed, they resettled in Kazakhstan and Kyrgyzstan and their families joined them. They found a job and work in recipient countries. Their status changed also. Now they live in the Central Asian countries not like refugees, but like citizens or labour migrants.

In the Caucasus, in 1995 the war for independence of the Republic of Chechnya (Ichheriya) against the Russian Federation erupted. The war was accompanied by a great loss of human life, destruction of cities and villages, damage to the country's economy and large-scale refugee movements from Chechnya to other CIS states, especially to Kazakhstan. It is understandable, that most of refugees from Chechnya fled to Kazakhstan. During the Second World War, thousands of Chechens were deported to Kazakhstan under the "special settlement" regime, on charges of alleged collaboration with the Nazis. After the Second World War, many Chechen deportees stayed in Kazakhstan, but not like "special settlers": they received equal rights with other ethnic groups of Kazakhstan. This explains why since 1995 Chechens found refuge in Kazakhstan where many of them joined to their relatives.

In the second half of 1993, the registered refugees in Kazakhstan were estimated to number about 1 million 751,000. The exact number of unregistered refugees is difficult to determine. As of 1995, the figures are as follows: the Office of the United Nations High Commissioner for Refugees and the Migration Department of the Republic of Kazakhstan estimate that 6,000 Chechen refugees have settled in Almaty, Atyrau, Mangystau, Karaganda, Kostanai, Aktubinsk, Pavlodar and Kokshetau oblasts. Refugees from

Afghanistan, numbering about 2,000, live primarily in the South: in Almaty, Jambul and Southern Kazakhstan oblasts. As for the refugees from Tajikistan, there are no reliable estimates. I would like to stress however, that these are official data, and that the real figures were probably much higher.

Ecological Refugees

Since 1991, Kazakhstan has been facing very serious ecological problems, especially with regard to the nuclear waste of the USSR. Parts of Kazakhstan have become ecological disaster zones, such as the Aral Sea and the Semipalatinsk nuclear testing site. Because of the shrinking of the Sea, the Aral Sea region in Kazakhstan, Karakalpakstan and Uzbekistan is experiencing chronic desertification and severe air, soil and water pollution. That is why, many people, mainly ethnic Kazakhs decided to return from Karakalpakstan to Kazakhstan. It has been estimated that in recent years some 95,000 people have left the region.

Apart from the ecological problems and financial difficulties of health care institutions, the situation is made worse by the fact that the Law of the Republic of Kazakhstan "On social protection of citizens suffering from the ecological disaster in the Aral Sea region", which should oversee the privileges available to women and children, has not been adequately implemented. Till 1999, there were 289 thousand ecological refugees in Kazakhstan. Since 2000, many ecological refugees (most of the Kazakhs and Karakalpaks) came to Kazakhstan from Uzbekistan. At the beginning of the 21st century, according to the United Nations High Commissioner for Refugees, 22.3 million people in the World were refugees. Among them 7.7 million refugees were in and from the former Soviet Union. Moreover, 1 million or more than 4 per cent of total World data were from Central Asia[12].

Brain Drain

The phenomenon of brain-drain for Central Asia began in early 1990s, when scientists and students were pushed with the circumstances working both in countries of donor, and in recipient countries. From home countries, they were "pushed out" by low incomes, a small demand, and not clear prospects[13]. In the West: EU, USA and Canada, they find not only higher standard of living but also respect for experts. Their adaptation is not so problematical, despite of language problems and difficulties of untraditional cultural environment[14].

For example, since 1990s, there are many Kazakh scholars, artists and musicians who left Kazakhstan for to work in the West, according to invitations of the Western governments and institutions. Since the early 1990s, the number of Central Asian scientists working abroad was approximately 30 thousand. I think that we need to put great attention to labour emigration of scientists as one of the channels of brain-drain, in order to solve the problem.

Labour Migration

The 1990s opened borders, which in combination with market-based reforms, mass unemployment and need to find new sources of income are the main reasons of intensification of labour migration in Central Asia. According to Independent Research Council on Migration in CIS and Baltic States data, about 10 million people – citizens of CIS countries formed part of the labour migration every year. Russian citizens constitute half of these migrants. Approximately, 1.5–2 million migrants from Russia get to work outside of CIS countries, about 3 million find work inside of Russia. At the same time, about 3 million migrants from CIS countries move to Russia and Kazakhstan for a job. Turkey, China, Korea, United Arabic Emirates, countries of the European Union, USA and Canada are the favourite directions of the external (foreign) labour migrants from Central Asia[15].

For example, we have voluntary migrations of the Kazakh Diaspora that can define as Labour, Cultural and Trade Diaspora. Today, the Kazakh Diaspora in the West consists of office employees in large corporations, hotels, and various other service industries. Many Kazakhs have their own businesses. About one third of them have manufacturing businesses in the Western European countries. Mass waves of migrants create problems in social-economical, political and cultural spheres of recipient-country: such as creating a burden on social infrastructure, intensification of business struggle, creation of migrant-phobias or xenophobia[16]. There are the negative aspects of migration.

Productive use of migrant's experience and skills both in donor and recipient countries, as well as, additional incomes to the economy of a state and family, are positive aspects of migration. For "pushing" countries, the positive elements are: decrease in the unemployment level; growth of money flow to the native country by migrant workers to their families and relatives; formation of the ethnic lobby in the accepting country acting in favour of the native state; and sometimes – even the support of this or that conflicting side. As for the "pulling" countries, the positive effect of migration is seen in the making up for the demographic resources, decreasing of the working force deficit, and others[17].

The flow of emigrants from countries of Central and Southeastern Europe, and from the former USSR in the West-European countries has grown. According to several International organizations, 172 million migrants are present in the World, from which 8–10 million accounts for Russia, and 12.5 million migrants – on the CIS countries[18].

Illegal Migration

Illegal migration[19] is more important and has influence on all situations in the Central Asian Region. As we know, illegal migration is accompanied by growing of criminalization of all spheres of life; promotion of corruption, stimulation of the increasing of "Shadow" (black, hidden) economy, etc. Violation of law takes place on various directions, such as naturalization, non-disclosure of taxation, smuggle, transit and distribution of drugs, etc. Moreover, illegal migration, refugee movements, traffic, human beings traffic and others are the sources of hidden threats, such as changing of demographic and social structure of population, diffusion (propagation) of infection diseases, etc.

In the Eurasian migratory system, the main migratory ways from Central Asia to the EU are passing through the Russian Federation, Ukraine and Belorussia. In Central Asia, Kazakhstan and Uzbekistan are the largest providers of migrants in Russia, Caucasus, Ukraine and Belorussia, and through them to the EU and further to the World. Kyrgyzstan and Tajikistan have migrants in Russia too, but their amount is not so considerable. Unfortunately, migration is used as the transit channel for trans-boundary criminal operations, such as drug industry (narcotic business), illegal migration, traffic in arms, trafficking etc., directed from the Asian countries on territory of the EU and America, in as in the opposite direction.

It's well-known, that illegal migration consists of four most important components:

1. Illegal entry to the country;
2. Illegal stay in the country;
3. Illegal employment; and
4. Illegal departure (exit) to another country that threatens to national security of any state[20].

After the collapse of the USSR the channel of carrying illegal migrants from countries of Southern and Eastern Asia (Afghanistan, Bangladesh, India, Iran, China, Pakistan, Sri Lanka, etc.) and even Africa through borders of China, Kyrgyzstan and Uzbekistan to border with Russia and further in the countries of the EU and America, was created. It is well-organized business of the transnational criminal groupings, skilfully using local conditions (the national legislation and system of International cooperation of the post-Soviet states of Central Asia). Penetration through reloading points is widespread. For example, from Sri Lanka illegal migrants depart to the United Arab Emirates, then to Kyrgyzstan and further to Kazakhstan. Through Kazakhstan, they follow by transit to Russia and further to the West.

For example, in 2007 in Almaty migratory police have

detained three citizens of the Islamic Republic of Pakistan, who have illegally crossed border of Kazakhstan with the purpose of the further moving to the countries of Europe. During investigation, it has been found out, that Italy was an ultimate goal of their travel. On the territory of our republic, they have got in illegally, without visas and came from Kyrgyzstan. According to the official data, about 80 per cent of illegal migrants enter Kazakhstan from Kyrgyzstan. According to data of the State Office of the Attorney-General of the Republic of Kazakhstan, growth of illegal migration is annually observed. "Economic development, public stability involves citizens of other states in our country. The stream of migrants increases every year", – the Attorney-General of the Republic of Kazakhstan has told. "Their no controllable arrival can negatively affect to our internal stability, and to become the reason of social tension"[21]. In such conditions it is necessary to examine what Kazakhstan and the Central Asian states can do to solve the problem of illegal migration?

Steps in Kazakhstan

In the summer of 2006 state action on legalization of illegal labour migrants began in Kazakhstan. It proceeds until now on realization of the law of RK "About amnesty in connection with legalization of illegal labour immigrants". In Kazakhstan, more than 300 thousand labour migrants were legalized. There are citizens of Uzbekistan – 160148, Kyrgyzstan – 25560, Russia – 11218 and Tajikistan – 4939 person among them. According to Ministry of Internal Affairs Republic of Kazakhstan, the greatest amount of immigrants is legalized in Almaty city, the Southern-Kazakhstan, Almaty and Mangystau oblasts[22]. Now a days, Kazakhstan tries to systematize the status of international labour migrants, to divide them on to three categories, such as international employees, season international employees, and business-immigrants. They will have different legal rights, recruitment standards, etc[23]. This project is now being discussed.

Therefore studying of this phenomenon is necessary both in scientific, and practical points of view. In that case, I would like to note, that in the Institute of Oriental Studies, Ministry of Education and Science of the Republic of Kazakhstan intensively carried out researches on the many-sided problems of migrations in the Central-Asian region. In 2006–2009 within the framework of fundamental researches, we have conduct research on the projects "Influence of Migrations on Development of the Central-Asian Region: Historical Aspect and Integration Prospects in 20–21st Centuries", and "Phenomenon of Migration in polyethnic Societies: in the Context of Creation of the National Idea of the Republic of Kazakhstan". It is thought, that joint efforts of scientists and practitioners of the Central-Asian region and International organizations can resolve the problems connected to illegal migration that should minimize threat of national and regional security.

Problems and their Solution and Perspectives

Another aspect of discussion concerns the solution of problems. Global migration flows are huge today[24]. Political and economic instability, demographic pressure, the formation of global labour market – all these are leading to the fact that today legal and illegal migration comprise more than 20 per cent of the population in more than 50 countries of the World. According to the data of the UN Department on Economic and Social Questions[25], in the mid-2010's there will be about 25.4 million international migrants in CIS countries. In 2010 in Kazakhstan international migrants will be an estimated 3.1 million people, in Uzbekistan – 1.2 million. Decreasing of international migrant's rate up to 10 per cent will take place in Kyrgyzstan. The official data till the end of 2009 registered, 6.3 per cent or 531.8 thousand people in Kazakhstan (7.9 million people were employees)[26] and 71.3 thousand persons in Kyrgyzstan.[27] Because of the World economic crisis, and various restrictions in some of the Central Asian countries the flow of legal migration decreased but illegal migration will increased in the region.

In order to change the situation in the region, the contemporary period has been characterized by the creation of coordinated measures of Kazakhstan, the Central Asian Republics, Russia, and the EU. If previously migration problems generally took the form of two-sided relations between countries, then now and in the future it will be dealing with many-sided and regional level. For example, cooperation of the EU and Central Asia focuses on prevention of illegal activities, such as corruption, money laundering, drugs and the prevention and control of illegal immigration. Similar coordinated measures between Central Asian and Southern Asian countries would move towards solving the problem.

The framework for EU relations with the Central Asian countries, Kazakhstan, Uzbekistan, Kyrgyzstan and Tajikistan, is provided by four bilateral Partnership and Cooperation Agreements[28], two important Tacis JLS-programs, one on borders and one on the fight against drugs; the *Border Management Initiative for Central Asia* (BOMCA) and the *Central Asia Drugs Action Programme* (CADAP)[29]. The PCA agreements cover fight against terrorism and drug trafficking, illegal activities, money laundering, illegal migration, asylum and readmission, as well as border control, customs and legislative cooperation.

In conclusion, it should be stressed that it is not easy to present all aspects of this problem. Nevertheless, it is clear that migrations in Central Asia have both positive and negative (aspects. In addition migration influences stability, national and regional security, and the integration of Central Asia to the World society.

Notes and References

1. Population Reference Bureau. *2009 World Population Data Sheet,* Washington, DC: Population Reference Bureau, 2009, p. 8.
2. Anita Sengupta, *Frontiers into Borders. The Transformation of Identities in Central* Asia, Hope India Publications/Greenwich Millennium, 2002.
3. UNHCR. *Refugees and Others of Concern to UNHCR in Countries of Commonwealth of Independent States (CIS) in 1999,* UNHCR, Geneva, 7 June 2000, p. 3/8. 2000. – Indicative number of refugees and others of concern to UNHCR, end 2000, UNHCR, *Provisional Statistics on Refugees and Others of Concern to UNHCR for the year 2000*, UNHCR, *Population Data Unit*, PGDS/UNHCR, Geneva, 11 April 2001, (www.unhcr/ch) tab. 1.; Gulnara Mendikulova, *Repatriation Into Kazakhstan: History and Current Situation.* International Conference on Central Asia. Toronto, 2000. # 6, pp. 77–81; Gulnara Mendikulova, "Some Problems of Adaptation of the Kazakh Repatriates (Oralmans) in Contemporary Kazakhstan". *Otan tarikhy,* 2004,

no 2: 3–35; Gulnara Mendikulova, Repatriation of the Kazakhs from Turkey into Sovereign Kazakhstan. *Interrelations of Turkey and Central Asia in the Context of Enlarging Europe*. Almaty, 2005. p. 257–266. (in Russian); Gulnara Mendikulova, *The Kazakh Diaspora: History and Modernity,* Almaty: Reiz, 2006 (Kazakhskaya diaspora: istoriya i sovremennost') (in Russian).

4. United Nations. *Population Division of the Department of Economic and Social Affairs of the United Nations Secretariat, Trends in Total Migrant Stock: The 2005 Revision* http://esa.un.org/migration. United Nations, POP/DB/MIG/Rev.2005. New York, 2006; Gulnara Mendikulova, *The Kazakh Diaspora: History and Modernity*; Gulnara Mendikulova, (2007). Illegal Migration in Kazakhstan as a Threat to National and Regional Security. (in Russian). *Proceeding International Conference "Afghanistan: 5 years after Taliban*", Dushanbe, 2006. pp. 67–79; Gulnara Mendikulova, *Illegal Migration in Central Asia as Destabilized Factor of the formation of National Idea in the Republic of Kazakhstan. Eastern Turkestan in Civilization Processes of Central Asia*. Almaty 2008 (forthcoming). (in Russian); and many others.
5. Agency on Statistics of the Republic of Kazakhstan. *Population Migration in the Republic of Kazakhstan*. Almaty: Agency on Statistics of the Republic of Kazakhstan, 2000; IOM. *Migration Trends in Eastern Europe and Central Asia. 2001–2002 Review*. Geneva: IOM, 2002; Gulnara Mendikulova, (2000). Repatriation Into Kazakhstan: History and Current Situation; Agency on Statistics of the Republic of Kazakhstan, *Demographical Annual Report of Kazakhstan in 2004. Statistical Reports*, Almaty: Agency on Statistics of the Republic of Kazakhstan, 2005. (in Russian).
6. Agency on Statistics of the Republic of Kazakhstan. *Population Migration in the Republic of Kazakhstan*. Almaty: Agency on Statistics of the Republic of Kazakhstan, 2000; IOM. *Migration Trends in Eastern Europe and Central Asia. 2001–2002 Review*. Geneva: IOM, 2002; Gulnara Mendikulova, *Repatriation Into Kazakhstan: History and Current Situation*; Agency on Statistics of the Republic of Kazakhstan. *Demographical Annual Report of Kazakhstan in 2004*. Statistical Reports. Almaty: Agency on Statistics of the Republic of Kazakhstan, 2005 (in Russian).
7. Law of the Republic of Kazakhstan about Migration (Zakon

Respubliki Kazakhstan ot 13 Dekabrya 1997 goda № 204-I. O Migratsii naseleniya. – Almaty, 1998. p. 121.

8. Gulnara Mendikulova, "Some Problems of Adaptation of the Kazakh Repatriates (Oralmans) in Contemporary Kazakhstan". *Otan tarikhy,* 2004, no 2: 3–35.
9. Mendikulova, 2000, 2004, 2005.
10. Agency on Statistics of the Republic of Kazakhstan *Statistical Yearbook of Kazakhstan,* Astana: Agency on Statistics of the Republic of Kazakhstan, 2007, pp. 26–28; *IA Novosti-Kazakhstan*, 18 January 2010. About *Oralmans* from China, please read in: Gulnara Mendikulova. *Contemporary Migration Trends between Kazakhstan and China, Proceeding of* International Conference "Central Asia-China: Conditions and Perspectives of Cooperation", 4–5th June 2008. Almaty: KISI, 2009. pp. 158–170.
11. United Nations High Commissioner for Refugees. *The State of the World's Refugees. In Search of Solutions*. United Nations High Commissioner for Refugees: Oxford University Press, 1995, pp. 24.
12. UNHCR. *Refugees and Others of Concern to UNHCR in Countries of Commonwealth of Independent States (CIS) in 1999.* UNHCR, Geneva, 7 June 2000, p. 3/8. 2000. – Indicative number of refugees and others of concern to UNHCR, end 2000 // Provisional Statistics on Refugees and Others of Concern to UNHCR for the year 2000, UNHCR, Population Data Unit, PGDS/UNHCR, Geneva, 11 April 2001, (www.unhcr/ch) tab. 1 pp. 3–8.
13. I.T. Katagotsina, "Intellectual Potential and Migratory Processes in the Central-Asian Region" (in Russian). *Vostok-Orient*, 1996, no 6: 70–88.
14. M. Beine, F. Docquier and H. Rapoport, "Brain Drain and Economic Growth: Theory and Evidence", *Journal of Development Economics* 64, (2001): 275–89; S. Blagov, "The Science Brain Drain", *InterPress Service,* 3 March, (2000) http://www.hartford-hwp.con/archives/63/339.html
15. Agency on Statistics of the Republic of Kazakhstan *Population Migration in the Republic of Kazakhstan.* Almaty: Agency on Statistics of the Republic of Kazakhstan 2000; Partnership and Co-operation Agreements (PCAs) (2003) http: // ec.europe.eu/ external_ relations/ceeca/pca/index.htm; Agency on Statistics of

the Republic of Kazakhstan *Demographical Annual Report of Kazakhstan in 2004. Statistical Reports*. Almaty Agency on Statistics of the Republic of Kazakhstan, 2005. (in Russian); IOM. *Migration Trends in Eastern Europe and Central Asia. 2001–2002 Review*. Geneva: IOM, 2002; IP/03/1017 - Brussels, 15 July 2003.

16. United Nations. *World Population Prospects. The 2004 Revision. Volume I* (United Nations publication, 2005. Sales No. E. 05.XIII. p. 5.
17. Mendikulova, 2008.
18. D. Pertsev, "Bored by Sun" (Utomlennye solntsem) (in Russian). *Gazeta.kz*. 2008, January 23.
19. G. Hanson, "The economic logic of illegal immigration", Council on Foreign Relations, Special Report, CSR # 26, 2007; IOM 2002; Agency on Statistics of the Republic of Kazakhstan. *Demographical Annual Report 2005*; Gulnara Mendikulova, 2007, 2008.
20. IOM, 2002, p. 38.
21. *Kazakhstan Today*, 25.01.08.
22. Mendikulova, 2008.
23. *IA Novosti-Kazakhstan*, 18 January 2010.
24. Population Reference Bureau. *2009 World Population Data Sheet*. Washington, DC, 2009. p. 8; OECD. *A Profile of Immigrant Populations in the 21st Century: Data from OECD countries*. Paris: OECD, 2008.
25. UN. *Trends In Total Migrant Stock: The 2008 Revision,* New York: UN, 2009.
26. *IA Novosti-Kazakhstan*, 12 January 2010.

27 CA-NEWS (KZ). 15-02-2008.

28. Partnership and Co-operation Agreements (PCAs).
29. Reuters (2005), ATHENS NEWS, 29/04/2005, page: A13 Article code: C13128A132; IP/03/1017 - Brussels, 15 July 2003.

Select Bibliography

Agency on Statistics of the Republic of Kazakhstan. *Demographical Annual Report of Kazakhstan in 2004. Statistical Reports*, Almaty: Agency on Statistics of the Republic of Kazakhstan, 2005. (in Russian).

Agency on Statistics of the Republic of Kazakhstan. *Population Migration in the Republic of Kazakhstan.* Almaty: Agency on Statistics of the Republic of Kazakhstan, 2000.

Agency on Statistics of the Republic of Kazakhstan. *Statistical Yearbook of Kazakhstan,* Astana: Agency on Statistics of the Republic of Kazakhstan, 2007.

S. Blagov, "The Science Brain Drain", *InterPress Service,* 3 March, (2000) http://www.hartford-hwp.con/archives/63/339.html.

M. Beine, F. Docquier and H. Rapoport, "Brain Drain and Economic Growth: Theory and Evidence", *Journal of Development Economics* 64, (2001): 275–89.

CA-NEWS (KZ). 15-02-2008.

G. Hanson, "The economic logic of illegal immigration", Council on Foreign Relations, Special Report, CSR # 26, 2007.

IA Novosti-Kazakhstan, 18 January 2010.

IOM. *Migration Trends in Eastern Europe and Central Asia. 2001–2002 Review*. Geneva: IOM, 2002.

IP/03/1017 - Brussels, 15 July 2003.

I.T. Katagotsina, "Intellectual Potential and Migratory Processes in the Central-Asian Region" (in Russian). *Vostok-Orient*, 1996, no 6: 70–88.

Kazakhstan Today, 25.01.08.

Law of the Republic of Kazakhstan about Migration (Zakon Respubliki Kazakhstan ot 13 Dekabrya 1997 goda № 204-I. O Migratsii naseleniya. Almaty, 1998. 121 p.

Gulnara Mendikulova. *Contemporary Migration Trends between Kazakhstan and China, Proceeding of* International Conference "Central Asia-China: Conditions and Perspectives of Cooperation", 4–5th June 2008. Almaty: KISI, 2009. p. 158–170.

___. *Illegal Migration in Kazakhstan as a Threat to National and Regional Security*. (in Russian). Proceeding International Conference "Afghanistan: 5 years after Taliban", Dushanbe, 2006. p. 67–79.

___. Illegal Migration in Central Asia as Destabilized Factor of the formation of National Idea in the Republic of Kazakhstan. Eastern Turkestan in Civilization Processes of Central Asia. Almaty 2008 (forthcoming). (in Russian).

____. *The Kazakh Diaspora: History and Modernity,* Almaty: Reiz, 2006 (in Russian). (Kazakhskaya diaspora: istoriya i sovremennost').

___. *Repatriation Into Kazakhstan: History and Current Situation.* International Conference on Central Asia. Toronto, 2000. # 6, pp. 77–81.

___. Repatriation of the Kazakhs from Turkey into Sovereign Kazakhstan. *Interrelations of Turkey and Central Asia in the Context of Enlarging Europe*. Almaty, 2005. pp. 257–266. (in Russian).

___. "Some Problems of Adaptation of the Kazakh Repatriates (Oralmans) in Contemporary Kazakhstan". *Otan tarikhy,* 2004, no 2: 3–35.

OECD. *A Profile of Immigrant Populations in the 21st Century: Data from OECD countries.* Paris: OECD, 2008.

Partnership and Co-operation Agreements (PCAs) (2003) http: // ec.europe.eu/external_relations/ceeca/pca/index.htm

D. Pertsev. *Utomlennye solntsem* (in Russian). *Gazeta.kz.* 2008, January 23.

Population Reference Bureau. *2009 World Population Data Sheet,* Washington, DC: Population Reference Bureau, 2009.

Reuters (2005), ATHENS NEWS, 29/04/2005, page: A13 Article code: C13128A132

Anita Sengupta, *Frontiers into Borders. The Transformation of Identities in Central* Asia, Hope India Publications/Greenwich Millennium, 2002.

UNHCR. *Refugees and Others of Concern to UNHCR in Countries of Commonwealth of Independent States (CIS) in 1999,* UNHCR, Geneva, 7 June 2000, p. 3/8. 2000. – Indicative number of refugees and others of concern to UNHCR, end 2000, UNHCR, *Provisional Statistics on Refugees and Others of Concern to UNHCR for the year 2000,* UNHCR, *Population Data Unit,* PGDS/UNHCR, Geneva, 11 April 2001, (www.unhcr/ch) tab. 1.

United Nations High Commissioner for Refugees. *The State of the World's Refugees. In Search of Solutions.* United Nations High Commissioner for Refugees: Oxford University Press, 1995.

United Nations. *Population Division of the Department of Economic and Social Affairs of the United Nations Secretariat, Trends in Total Migrant Stock: The 2005 Revision* http://esa.un.org/ migration (United Nations, POP/DB/MIG/Rev.2005), 2006.

United Nations. *Trends In Total Migrant Stock: The 2008 Revision,* New York: UN, 2009.

United Nations. *World Population Prospects. The 2004 Revision. Volume I.* United Nations publication, 2005.

5

Migration: Impact on Asiatic Russia

P.L. Dash

Hard to believe that 70 percent of the world population live along the sea shores on a patch of land extending just 300 kilometres inland from the sea coast. More so half of this 70 percent population resides worldwide just along a stretch of 100 kilometres inward from sea shore.[1] Those who fail to get to the sea shores look for exotic locations along lakes and rivers. Land locked regions are the least preferred areas of human habitat. Therefore we see concentration of industry along the sea shores and consolidation of business along the cities that attract labour migrant to urban industrial centres. While this human proclivity has been intensely validated throughout history, a tangible aberration was the Soviet migration pattern. The human preference normally falls on the place, where one could get, aside from aquatic attraction, a better living standard accompanied by facilities for a healthy and comfortable living. However, the Soviets controlled this human preference and arranged migration of the people where the state required them the most. Through the Soviet years migration had invariably taken place to five Soviet republics: Russia, the Ukraine, and the three Baltic states of Lithuania, Latvia and Estonia. However, migration was a terminology unheard of in Soviet years. This was simply because Moscow controlled all population movements in the country.

Beginning late 1980s, in response to Gorbachev's *perestroika* and *glasnost* and subsequently following Soviet disintegration the situation radically altered. The state control began paving way to free movement of people for permanent settlement. Control further dissipated with the advent of globalisation and successor countries of the Soviet Union experienced something incredible, which they had never witnessed earlier. People could move and work freely was a choice no longer bestowed with the state. Imperatives arose that economies in the vast swathe of Russian landmass must open themselves to the outside world and ought to integrate into the world economic system. This did not happen in a big way, resulting across the post-Soviet space in a tumultuous process of unregulated migration of people, some with legal documents, still others without documents, many with the passport of a country that no longer existed and many with no clear objectives. What allured them was the novelty of economic transformations. Economic development at this phase was closely linked to availability of qualified cadres at the required place; and despite a massive population movement throughout the CIS, these cadres remained continually unavailable, precipitating the urgency for accommodating labour migrants in labour deficit, industrial areas. Russia, however, remained the magnet in the CIS that attracted people from all over the post-Soviet prefectures and abroad. As revealed by the 2002 census data, net migration impact on the Russian population was insignificant – an addition of 5.6 million people because during the post-Soviet years 11 million immigrated to Russia of which 5.4 million had emigrated.[2]

The post-Soviet population movement has been one of most traumatic episodes of mankind in recent memory. In the immediate aftermath of the Soviet collapse, when one country became fifteen, and within the Russian Federation 89 autonomies so constituted themselves as to be administered by Moscow, people looked forward to moving out of state control as and when they got an opportunity. However, this did not occur exactly as people wished. State intervention remained a potential meddling factor at a time of chaotic transition all over the post Soviet space. This choice was varied. Some moved for better prospects, others to get rid of inhospitable climate, still others to unite with their kith and kin, yet still others to settle in urban centres and so on. The state had now no control over who moved from where to where. As a result, it was revealed by the census in 2002 that 13,000 villages in far flung Asiatic Russia had altogether vanished because its people moved to salubrious climate and hospitable townships that could provide them a comfortable life style and jobs. There was no record available about the closure of another 2000 villages. Thus migration instantly was related to so many things: job prospects, life style, urbanisation, availability of better opportunities and infrastructures, compulsive family requirements, desire to unite with ethic brethrens and so on. However, the dislocation of entire families, who left their place of residence lock, stock and barrel due to a suddenly emerging hostile surroundings, resulting from ethnic squabbles in quest for a new place of settlement was too disheartening. Dislocation brought with it displacement and this had created too many social and economic problems for the authorities and the émigrés to handle, This paper aims at analysing and highlighting a few important aspects of the population movement in Russia in general and Asiatic Russia in particular through the years following the Soviet sunset.

Pattern and Causes

Migration in the Soviet years to Asiatic Russia was done in a systematic manner. When in the 1930s, the success of experimenting with the Soviet five year plans overwhelmed European Russia, beyond the Urals, save few urban centres, its impact was insignificant. With exploration of oil and gas in the late 1950s and 1960s, need arose to set up urban centres close to the places where these discoveries were made. That's how people began migrating to Asiatic part of the Russian Federation to work in state owned oil firms. Migrants poured in from all over the Soviet Union, but in a regulated fashion. The increasing demand of accommodation to settle them required all sorts of workers – from highly qualified technical cadres to job seekers as labourers. The trend continued throughout the 1970s in the Asiatic part, when the Baikal-Amur rail line was built. Even students, including foreign students, were requisitioned from all higher educational institutes from across the country to work in this construction project during their summer vacations, while throughout the former USSR student labour was variously used for plucking fruits and harvesting potatoes.

The post-Soviet migration threw up different patterns of peacetime movement of people, not restricted by too many legal encumbrances. The notion of freedom of movement got corroborated, when in the aftermath of the Soviet collapse, unrestricted migration across republics swept many families to opt for an alternative place of residence. This was the spate of voluntary migration that had driven in droves thousands of ethnic non-natives from Central Asia. Most of them were sent by the state to Central Asia in the past to help the region economically develop. And these are migrants, who do not wish to go back to the republics where they were settled for decades. Once back in homeland, they have found their roots in their eponymous republics. These are migrants conditioned by circumstances and compelled by the apprehensions of possible ethnic reprisals.

The second category is the involuntary, non-native migrants, who wish to stay in the place of their residence, but circumstantial persuasion compels them to move out. They wish not to sever their ties with the region with a sincere hope that Russia might one day come back to rule. In the absence of dual citizenship and clear laws about status of non-native nationalities, the involuntary migrants find their family dislocated – wife living with her parents, hubby in the army serving elsewhere, mother in the village living by herself and father, separated from mother by divorce, lives in his native place and children studying in different places in higher educational institutes somewhere in the post Soviet space. Such phenomenon of disarray is a typical manifestation of peacetime family dislocations with varied social ramifications across the CIS. A family reunion is an impossible proposition in such a situation because all cannot unite at a given place on a given day.

The third type of migrants is workforce migrants – job seekers, who move to any part of the globe in search of employment. The Central Asian job seekers have thronged primarily to Russian cities for employment and secondarily to the Ukraine because the labour market is big, demand for workforce has been steadily increasing, salary structure is better and money transfer easier. Further, the reasons are as much geographical proximity to home as language savvy area. Such migrants constitute nearly 1.6 million people alone in the Russian Federation and all of them are illegal aliens from the countries of near abroad although they work in legal and quasi-legal jobs.

The fourth factor is law induced migration. In post-Soviet Central Asia such laws were language laws that emphasized the primacy of the native language in each Central Asian country. Although Russian continues to remain the language of intercommunication at the supranational level, what has overwhelmed the national and sub-national scenario is the increasing inclination to assert the primacy of republican languages. The adoption of laws about medium of instructions in educational institutions in favour of the native language, replacing Russian and legislations about the native language to be used as official language have induced instant migration proclivity among the non-natives. It is an irony to note that the natives of Central Asia were forced to learn the Russian language throughout the Soviet years, while the Russians never cared to learn the language of other countries, and that showed lackadaisical attitude by the Russians to a highly sensitive and emotive issue such as the language.

The fifth reason that transpires migratory inclination to change place of residence is the fear factor and the worries about national identity. Fear of repression in a place of ethnic volatility, apprehensions about extreme politicization of related aspects of ethno-nationalism such as nativity, religion, language, culture and so on, and above all systematic economic deprivation in the job market are potent causes to encourage emigration. These are not only the worries and fears of those affected people, but also fears and worries of the host country. For example, in the early 1990s, two third of the migrants in Europe were Muslims and population growth in Europe was virtually zero. Muslims accounted for 10 percent all births in Europe, thereby generating concerns about Muslims overwhelming European demography in foreseeable future. The Europeans increasingly fear that they are now being invaded not by armies and tanks, but by migrants, who "speak other languages, worship other Gods, and belong to other cultures." Russia's European population vis-à-vis Central Asia's Muslim population is not dissimilar.

Finally, in volatile areas, illegal migration has formed alliance with various criminal gangs to derive benefits. Criminalization of migration process is a systematic endeavour to involve migrants in the criminal nexus of narcotic trafficking, small arms trade, money laundering and human trafficking. A case in point with regard to illegal human trafficking was noticed when "in December, 2005 the Russian Coast Guard discovered 25 Ukrainian men on a Russian fishing boat in the Sea of Japan. On promise of good pay, they were lured aboard industrial fishing vessels, when they were found exhausted, half-starved and locked on the ship's hold. Their passport had been taken away and they has been forced at gun point to work extremely long hours with no pay at all."[3] This shows the endemic nature of the problem. And women trafficking for prostitution and domestic labour are a big social issues under debate by sociologists. Human trafficking happens in connivance with corrupt officials, who handle migration cases. Geographical proximity of Russia with Kazakhstan and Kyrgyzstan is used as the main highway of all illegal activities. All criminal elements form a nexus that is too hard to crack. Along this route, illegal migration from Central Asia and from other foreign countries to Russia has been steadily rising. From just 60,000 foreigners in 1997, who passed via Kazakhstan to Russia from Central Asia, the number rose to 730,000 in 2002 to 817,000 in 2003 and almost 970,000 in 2005. Most recent figures may be still higher. Interestingly, from September 1999, some 27,600 Chechens have passed through the Kazakh cities of Alma-Ata, Astana, Karaganda, Akhmola and South Kazakhstan Oblasts, where Kazakh Chechens are compactly settled.[4]

A point to further ponder is the specific situation prevailing in Tajikistan. As the only country that passed through the post-Soviet chaos of a civil war resulting from regional, factional rivalry, Tajikistan served as a cauldron of problems that a newly independent country could anticipate to pass through. Close to Afghanistan and with the Pyandz river diving the border, it remained the major heroin highway of narcotic trafficking to Russia and beyond. And a civil war like situation suited all those involved in that lucrative trade. It was in this situation that natives and non-natives both chose emigration as the only escape route to freedom. A survey conducted by a Tajik NGO and published by Asia Plus information agency revealed that around 80 percent of young Tajik were inclined to migrate from Tajikistan to Russia. While this is the general mentality among the youngsters, it has been unofficially reported that during peak of seasonal work, some 1 million Tajik youth go to Russia to work, which means every fifth citizen is looking positively at migration as a means to livelihood. This figure is in consonance with the overall regional figure of 10 out of 50 million people migrating from the region. The poorer the country, the higher is the propensity to emigrate. The overall regional picture implies something like: mostly from Tajikistan, moderately from Kyrgyzstan and Uzbekistan and least from Kazakhstan and Turkmenistan because the latter two countries are relatively more prosperous than the former three. Kazakhstan has recently become a host country for migrants and Turkmenistan has not adequately opened up to host migrants except in the massive construction sector that is contracted mostly to Turkish real estate firms. Even in the fluid years of Perestroika, the tendency to emigrate took roots and there was no dearth of people willing then to migrate to Russia. Russian sources cited that between 1989, when ethnic violence in Osh took place and 1992, when Central Asian countries entered into the first year of independence the migration figures from central Asia to Russia were: 143,400 from Uzbekistan, 127,900 from Kazakhstan, 65,600 from Tajikistan, 43,900 from Kyrgyzstan, and 14,300 from Turkmenistan.[5]

Social Impact

Once this mass movement of people took place, there was a distinct cultural clash. When people, whose social conditioning had been religiously determined by Islam, chose to migrate to areas where Islam is not practised, they faced a different socio-cultural milieu. This fact must not escape sight while analysing migration issues and displacement implications in Asiatic Russia. Plus it must be remembered that population movement in the past was designed by a political system completely alien to Islam. The complexity of the mentality of migrants and their mindset discernibly mismatched with the intentions of the state. And the varied socio-cultural background of the migrants created a problem for adjustment in the new place of settlement. This happened, particularly with those who migrated from Uzbekistan, Tajikistan and Kyrgyzstan. Given that the overall cultural environment remained static, the migrants from the Islamic zone faced the challenge of adapting to the Russian Orthodoxy if they migrate to European Russia. Should their preference to migrate fall on Asiatic Russia, they largely confronted Buddhism along the border areas with China and Mongolia – a different religion with much different practices and ethos and very much dissimilar to Islam. Thus in a social sense, there is a clear mismatch of attitude conditioned by different religions that have determined the tradition, the mores and rites, religious practices, social behaviour, attitude to life and so on. The migrants became thus other people from other religion and other region that bestows on them alien status forever.

To comprehend this complex process of how empirically societies interface with one another one must understand the theoretical interplay of factors that influence their lives in the society. The social impact is the outcome of the interface people encounter with various other factors. They included ethno-national, ethno lingual, ethno-cultural, ethno-political and several other social categories. Russian researcher, P.V. Chernov, analyzing the complexity of "geoethno-sociopolitical" terminology adduced five possible variables for studying socially conflict ridden situation that culminated invariably in migration. They include:

1. Geo-ethno-socio-political;
2. Ethno-geo-socio-political;
3. Socio-ethno-geo-political;
4. Geo-socio-ethno-political;
5. Ethno-socio-geo-political.[6]

While political aspects worked in Chernov's theory as fulcrum and other three variables intertwined with one another, the tangible conclusion one could deduce was the interaction of all these elements in potentially hostile surroundings, particularly in the context of cross border settlements. Geo means land, ethno means people and socio means society. In any form of governance, politics crop up as a potential moderating force between these elements. However, Chernov did not include three other potential divisive elements and one more overarching cohesive element that strangely interact in such situations. He could have included cultural and linguistic and confessional aspects as potential divisive factors, wrecking the post-Soviet space, particularly Central Asia and Asiatic Russia, posing a major source of immigration to Russai. Logically that tends us to include three other conceivable variables such as 1. Geo-ethno-socio-linguo-political, 2. Socio-religious-ethno-geo-political and 3. Geo-cultural-religious-ethno-political to the gamut of debates that precipitated emigration en masse.

While the addition of linguistic, religious and cultural elements to the displacement process tends to give the displaced persons a leverage to balance their activities at any given place, in any given society, all eight elements are together inevitable essentialities of a harmonious society. Any imbalance among them would result in a tilt either in favour of harmony or disharmony, depending on how a particular ethnic group behaves in a multi-ethnic society. Since all peoples, at all times, in all countries and in all situations have to engage themselves in economic activities to earn a livelihood, it is essentially the economic sphere encompassing economic activities and interactions among groups that provide a cushion to harmonizing social relationship. This is why politics is so intricately linked to viable economic policy. The weaker the economy, the more volatile is politics, and in the case of weakness of both economic policy and political governance, the situation becomes pregnant with hostility and mutual animosity, thereby threatening non-natives, and in some cases natives too, to leave their homeland. Political instability and economic uncertainty are combustible combination in the former Soviet space of Asiatic Russia to have triggered fear among non-autochthonous nationalities to quit their place of residence.

Practical Implications

Away from theory, the post-Soviet practice offers fascinating facts about migration. First of all, when thousands of villages entirely disappeared in Asiatic Russia without knowledge of the state, this clearly showed freedom had worked. People voluntarily migrated to the nearest city centres for permanent settlement the moment they got a chance to buy land build house and settle. After the census data were collected, the Russian authorities began wondering for a while how and where to locate its residents in those missing villages. They were located, but in other places from where they were unwilling to return to their place of Soviet era residence.

Secondly, Russia has few attractive cities. Baring Moscow and St. Petersburg, it has just eleven other cities across eleven time zones of the country with a population of one million or more.[7] The tenacity to cling to places that could provide the comforts of modern life against the desire of a state that was always prepared to migrate people where resources could be exploited created a situation in which migration seemed a planned effort on the part of the state and coercive deportation for those who migrated, albeit under certain pecuniary inducements that was otherwise unavailable to them.

Thirdly, while these were the normal extant situation with regard to the migrants, what was undesirable was seemingly unpalatable. Given that migrants are in disarray in their new place of residence, the mafia and the criminals took advantage of their presence and recruited them for every sort of activity that was not licit. From construction work to narcotic trafficking, prostitution and human trafficking, extortion and pillage to terror acts migrant population indulged in multifaceted human endeavour to earn their livelihood in their new place of residence. And this created a real problem for the state to handle. Registering migration in vast Russia was a Herculean task for the state, particularly in Asiatic Russia, where illegal Chinese migrants outnumbered all other migrants put together. This changed the configuration of Russian demography, where European Russia stood in stark contrast with Asiatic Russia.

Finally, in the global context, Asiatic Russia seemed a demographic contrast: close to the rising Asia, where China, Japan, India, and other South East Asian countries were showing remarkable economic progress vis-à-vis Europe languishing with no tangible growth to its credit. Asiatic

Russia and the East further provided hopes due to their enormous natural resource endowment that required manpower for exploitation. And this in turn facilitated migration of labour force from areas of luxurious population growth to areas of scanty growth. Asiatic Russia belonged to the last category, while its neighbour China belonged to the former category. Some significant developments single out Russia in the global demographic context. In the immediate periphery of Russia, in the Asia and the Pacific, live half of the world's total population. China and India are home to 2.3 billion of the world's total of 6.1 billion people. Its southern surroundings, awash with luxuriant population growth, Russia in the upcoming decades would seem like a massive desert semi-circled by an oasis. Yet two global demographic tendencies are mirrored in the Russian predicament. First, European Russia has become a part of the universal aging process, sweeping the globe, while Asian and Caucasian parts remain the mainstay of relatively younger population. Secondly, fertility decline and high mortality rate are equally akin to what is happening elsewhere in Europe and America. This would mean that in future Russia would depend more on migrant population than native Russians to meet the labour requirement of the country.

It is for the first time at the turn of this century that global aging, fertility decline and mortality increase have become widespread phenomena. The related dimensions of the luxury of aging and having small nucleus families have raised many ethical issues and responsibilities to be addressed by governments and societies in different countries. It is not ironical that 1999 was observed by the United Nations as the "Year of the Older Person".[8] Older people too need younger ones to look after them. And that very requirement would trigger migration.

While the issue awaits a separate, universal debate on old age, nucleus families and population growth, critical and practical component are those that tend to underscore in the Russian context the very fact that global demographic changes are likely to influence Russia in general and Asiatic Russia in particular in the foreseeable future. Should Russia choose to adopt a migrant savvy population policy, the migration inflow to Russia will be largely, and unexpectedly from the Asia Pacific countries rather than from European countries. The pivotal location of Russia in Central Eurasia makes her vulnerable to excessive cross-breeding, resulting in synthesis and assimilation of nations, and leading finally to extinction of some of them.

A contrasting demographic contour of Europe,·largely having older population, and Asia possessing youngsters would throw open the challenge for Russia who to choose between. And surely younger Asian labour force, educated and talented in India and China, would be an obvious preference to older European labourers, who cost more. There is also another contrast: India has more younger population than China. 35 percent of Indians are below 35 years of age, while the Chinese population is relatively aged. But China has numerical superiority for the time being that, demographers predict, would tilt in India's favour in a decade or two. In addition India and China are two countries home to one sixth of the world population, implying that every sixth citizen of the world lives either in China or in India. These are the two countries with huge labour market. India's English savvy, educated middle class youth may throw up an engaging challenge to the Chinese labour force in Asiatic Russia in the years to come. This contrast is dampened by China's contiguity to Russia. Russia's porous Asiatic borders further facilitate illegal migration from China to Russia, while Indians would wait for the legal channel.

The opening up of the Russian market in the context of globalization had brought in foreign workers to Russia from across all continents. They came from Asia and Africa, many thousand asylum seekers from Afghanistan, China, Iraq, Sri Lanka Somalia, Angola, Ethiopia and Zaire. Most of these workers have had temporary work permits with impermanent stay permit. They apparently wished to make Russia a transit home before they finally migrated to Western Europe. But their number has been gradually swelling, and this is once again no tangible addition to Russia's population growth. In April, 1996 Boris Yeltsin had admitted that there were 180,000 illegal migrants from China, mostly living in the Khabarovsk territory,[9] but their number over the past decade has swelled to millions. The Russian authorities find the Chinese migrants in their Far Eastern part as a formidable problems to deal with.

A noteworthy feature of the Chinese migrants is that many of them are ethnic Koreans; but Chinese citizens, who could be legitimately called Korean Chinese emigrants. In that part of the Russian world, their ethnic features are similar to those of the local people, thereby making them physically indistinguishable. In fact, a lot of ethnic Koreans have been living in the former Soviet space for ages. A survey had revealed that in 1999, Russia had 125,000 ethnic Koreans, Ukraine had 9,000, Uzbekistan had 198,000, Kazakhstan had 105,000, Kyrgyzstan had 19,000, Tajikistan had 6,000,

Turkmenistan had 3,000 and other republics had 5,000.[10] Since most of these ethnic Koreans were located in Central Asia, Kazakhstan and Russian Federation, inclination for congregation must have driven them to places of their choice in Asiatic Russia, presumably because that part of Russia is less crowded and more resource rich than other places that could provide job opportunities in future. In addition, by moving to Asiatic Russia, these ethnic Korean Chinese migrants will be closer to their native Koreans than they could have been from any other location. And this would provide them with a sense of human security and native ethnic belongingness. Certainly, the desire to cling to the eponymous ethno-cultural roots has had more priority than the desire to settle down in a place surrounded by aliens, who could prove ethnically hostile.

Besides, labour has a tendency to migrate from less developing regions to relatively prosperous areas, precipitating the challenge for Russia to streamline her own internal population dynamics, first within Russian Federation; secondly within the post-Soviet space; and thirdly choose between the emerging demographic lines of migration, no matter whether from Asia or Europe or from China or India. Asiatic Russia would remain a labour deficit area and import of labour is a practical problem facing the region with it huge resources awaiting exploitation. The ball is in the court of the Kremlin to introduce labour savvy policies so as to suit Russian national interest and population growth, and at the same time, facilitate rational use of Asiatic resources, including human resources available in neighbouring countries.

Central Asian Conduit

Migration to the Russian Federation would continue in foreseeable future. Relative to Asiatic Russia, larger flow would come from the Central Asian countries, medium flow from the Caucasian underbelly and mild flow from the European part. Migration also has a tendency to favour stable and liberal regime that would not create impediments for peoples' movement. Kazakhstan is therefore the place, the hub through which large migration takes place, both to Asiatic and European Russia. From all countries of Central Asia as well as from China massive migration has been taking place via Kazakhstan because major railways and highways from Central Asia lay through that country. During the post-Soviet years, some 11 plus million refugees have come to Russia with the intention of permanently settling down. In 66 of the 89 regions of the Russian Federation, population figures have come down. The Far East has "lost 16 percent of its population. In Yaroslavl and Bologod oblasts, entire villages are empty. 8 percent of villages in Russia have been depopulated. Increase is noticed only in the southern regions."[11] Thus a continuously dwindling population throughout the Russian Federation coupled with a sustainable growth of population in the Southern Muslim underbelly in Caucasus and Central Asia is another sinister development for Russian authorities to ponder over. The moot point that needs to be underscored from a demographer's view point was that their contribution to population growth would have been larger had they lived in peace rather than in fear of ethnic war. Yet, net contribution of migrants to Russia's population growth has been approximately 45–50 thousand children, born of migrant parents, who are now Russian citizens. An analysis of Russian emigration and immigration data reveal that migrants have added 2.7 million people to the country's population.[12]

Central Asia, and particularly Kazakhstan that serves as Russia's gateway southward, would be a tangible source of migration to Asiatic Russia. Within the Russian Federation, as per the 2002 census, ethnic Russians comprised of 79.83 percent of the population followed by Tatars, a Muslim population scattered from Crimea to the Russian eastern flank, but compactly concentrated in Tatarstan and comprising just 3.83 percent of the total Russian population. The gap is too glaring to be too easily filled by any singular migrant community.[13] Thus in the upcoming years, as the sway of globalization would sweep Russia, the Russians would stand at the base of a migration pyramid, controlling from below all movements of people on the vast landmass of the Russian Federation and effectively engaging them in various spheres of human endeavour.

Notes and References

1. Ahmed Kurmanov, 'Silk Route without Kazakhstan', *Russia and the Muslim World,* No. 3, 2005, p. 162 reproduced from Respublika, Alma Ata, 26 November, 2004.
2. Based on Russia Census Report, see P. L. Dash, 'Russia: The Demographic Danger' in Shashikant Jha and Bhaswati Sarkar (ed.) *Amidst Turbulence and Hope, Transition in Russia and Eastern Europe*, Lancer, New Delhi, 2002.
3. 'Silent Servants: Human trafficking fuels economies, Destroys Lives', *Asia Pacific Defence Forum*, Vol. 33, No. 3, 2008, p. 46.
4. Gulmira Arbabaeva, 'Kazakhstan: The Burden of Illegal Emigration', *Russia and the Muslim World*, No. 8, 2005, p. 159.

5. *Post-Sovietskaya Tsentral'naya Aziya: Poterii i Obreteniya, pod redaktsii A.M. Vasiliyeva*, Moscow, 1998, p. 118.
6. P.V. Chernov, *Rossiya: Etnopoliticheskie Osnobi Gosudarstvennosti, Vostochnaya Literatura*, Moscow, 1999, p. 19.
7. The cities with more than one million population were Nizhnyi Novgorod, Rostov na Donu, Volgograd, samara Kazan, Ufa, Perm, Yekaterinburg, Chelyabinsk, Omsk and Novorossisk. There were 65 other cities across Russia where the population figure varied between 50 to 100 to 200 thousand people. Please refer to Results of the All Russian Population Census, Goskomstat, Moscow, 2002.
8. Kevin Kinsella, 'Demographic Dimensions of Global Aging', *Journal of Family Issues*, Vol. 21, July, 2000, No. 5, p. 541.
9. Population Movements in Countries of the Commonwealth of Independent States, *Foreign and Commonwealth Office background Brief*, London, July 1996.
10. Jean Young Lee, 'Korean Chinese Migration into Russian Far East: A Human Security Perspective', in Iwashita Akihiro (Ed.) *Siberia and the Far East in the 21st Century: partners in the Community of Asia*, Slavic Research Centre, Hokkaido University, Sapporo, 2005, p. 73.
11. Census 2002, *Argumenty i Fakty*, No. 18, 2003, p. 5.
12. V. Kokov, 'Kak Ypravlyat' Migratsiei Rossii', *Ekonomist*, No. 2, 2002, p. 79.
13. Should we Parade our Nationalities? A Roundtable Proceedings published in *Russia and the Muslim World*, No. 8, 2005, p. 15.

6

Migration as a "Factor of Vulnerability" for Central Asian Integration

Kamilla Sheryazdanova

Solving problems related to the process of migration is the most important function of state policy in Central Asian region today. Attention is due to the problem of migration for external and internal reasons. In the modern world migration occurs due to economic development, interchange of progressive technologies and knowledge and the intersection of cultures. At the same time, processes of external migration may be accompanied by such negative consequences as brain drain, loss of finance from Kazakhstan citizens, being emigrants or working abroad, development of criminal structures specializing in illegal supply of man power to neighbouring or far foreign countries, increase of scope of illegal migration, etc. Integration of CAR countries to the international labour market should be conducted with proper observation towards state interests. However, insufficient development of common state and regional strategy in the sphere of migration policy negatively influences on many aspects of practice in CAR countries connected with the management of these processes.

Illegal migration is arrival (departure) from one country to another, not permitted by the authorities of one party or of both parties. Clandestine or illegal labour migrations are the actions of persons, departing to tour or to visit relatives and working without Agreement or Contract after the expiry dates of entrance visa, not protected by Labour or other Legislation of accepting party[1]. Illegal migration is often connected with the employment agencies abroad masking well-arranged business in human traffic. Modern migration processes in CAR are connected with the whole complex of reasons. For external migration, the dominating event is the combination of social-economical and political factors, and for inter-republic migration – social-economical and ecological factors. Dissolution of CIS intensified crisis situation in economy, being accompanied by setback in production, inflation growth, unemployment increase; and this led to the reduction of living standard of people and crisis condition of social sphere.

Population migration from CAR greatly influenced the number and the structure of population of local republics. Migration damaged economy and demographic situation, given the fact that the people who departed from the republics were generally people with higher education, qualified and certified specialists, young and able-bodied and of non-native nationalities. The level of illegal migration especially increased in 1990s in Kazakhstan. Potential factors of the increase in migration flow were regional instability and military conflicts in Afghanistan and Tajikistan, military actions in the Northern Caucasus, drug-traffic from Afghanistan. According to the estimations of the experts, about two thirds of drugs are produced in Afghanistan and about 70 per cent of them are transported through CAR countries[2].

The enormous extension of boundaries and their relative openness was one of the reasons for the increase in illegal migration and appearance of transit channels of human traffic. This situation is so very urgent that all CAR Republics are included in so called the third list of countries composing problem zones and insufficiently ability to fight this negative phenomenon. The facts that full registration of the foreigners arriving and crossing the territory of the republics via transit is not recorded and state border is not secured along the entire border further complicates this situation. In spite of acceptance of normative-legal documents regulating states' fight with illegal migration, legislative base does not correspond to the current situation.

Under the estimation of International Migration Organization (IMO), just in Kazakhstan more than 19 thousand refugees was registered by 2004[3] Refugees are the emigrants from CIS (Tajikistan, Chechnya, etc.), nevertheless, they dominate among forced migrants to Kazakhstan: accordingly, 5 thousand or 24 per cent and 12.6 thousand people or 62 per cent form the total number of forced migrants. Procedure of re-registration is not always observed by them, and so they are considered to be infringers[4].

China is one of so called "suppliers" of illegal migrants. Intensive immigration of the Chinese to CAR took place from the beginning of 1990s when bilateral relations began to develop and as a result trade contacts near the boundary zone and "shop-tourism" became significant. According to the data of boundary services, from 1990s, for example, 150–200 Chinese tourists daily arrived in Kazakhstan, among whom 30–50 did not return to China. Unregulated arrival of the great number of Chinese citizens to the Republic of

Kazakhstan caused intensification of the crime situation. As a result during negotiations non-visa regime of mutual trips was established only for the holders of diplomatic and official passports. Till the middle of 1999, transit migration from China highlighted the absence of serious control at the Southern borders of Kazakhstan with Turkmenistan, Uzbekistan, and Kyrgyzstan After armed conflicts in Kyrgyzstan, authorities arranged check points at the borders with these countries. Nevertheless, passing of the border is carried out without any difficulties as before.

According to the opinion of Ye. Yu. Sadovskaya, non-visa regime, higher level of salary and favourable economical current situation attracts low-cost manpower from the republics of Central Asia to the Republic of Kazakhstan. According to the estimation of the experts, in Almaty and Zhambyl regions there are about 50 thousand illegal labour migrants from Kyrgyzstan and Uzbekistan (in agriculture, production, construction). There is an agrarian migration of the Uzbek to the Southern Kazakhstan Region, several thousand of the Uzbeks are working in the bordering regions of the Republic of Kazakhstan. The number of labour migrants from Tajikistan is about 50 thousand people[5]. Migration also takes place at the border with Russia. People are moving from satellite towns to the industrial cities of Siberia. "Shuttle" migration is most common.

On the whole, the scope of illegal migration undoubtedly influences the national labour markets of CIS countries. Moreover, such negative phenomena as trade in arms, drugs, people accompanies this problem. Adequate legal base and intimate contact of state bodies of the region, as MIA, CNS, MEA, etc., are necessary for solving the problems of illegal migration. It is noteworthy, that at the Russian-Kazakhstan borders in 1999 Russian Services seized more than 90 per cent of all drugs seized at all borders of Russia. The network of criminal business includes corrupted officials from MIA, MEA, Consulates of foreign embassies. So, during two-year investigation, according to the opinion of B. Hallist, amalgamation of criminal organizations and state bodies took place in many countries of the former USSR[6].

The problem of "traffic" of women and children is another social danger. This problem was unexplored till recently. Nowadays, traffic belongs to the group of transnational organized crimes and this means that the fight against them requires strict coordinated measures mobilizing all forces of the society. According to the definition, accepted during Transnational Labour seminar on illegal traffic of women held in Budapest city in 1988: "Illegal traffic of people (Trafficking) is all actions connected with engaging for work or transportation of people inland and abroad, including fraud, compulsion, with the purpose of putting people into humiliating labour conditions, such as forced prostitution, practice like slavery, beating and extreme cruelty, slave labour, kidnapping, illegal or arbitrary deprivation of freedom, forced labour and other actions, which violate the main rights of a man"[7].

In 2000, for instance, the first investigation on traffic was conducted in Kazakhstan by Crisis Center for women and children of RK, which established that 91 per cent of women ready to go abroad may become potential victims due to their incompetence, lack of legal protection and ignorance[8]. But the principal reasons of macro-order are defects of state policy, instability and corruption. Imperfection of legislative acts, absence of articles in criminal legislation on traffic led to difficulty in bringing the criminals to legal liability. In 2001, in Almaty the first Central Asian conference on traffic was oganized "Traffic of people: information as prevention" with the support of Informational Service of USA Embassy, where representatives of 5 republics of CAR, members of National Commission on family and women affairs under the President of RK, representatives of international organizations took part.

It was decided at the conference that state policy regulating flows of the migrants is necessary to fight with illegal migration. State bodies are to create proper conditions for legal departure of citizens for work to other countries, and that it is necessary to consider the problem of traffic more broadly, from the point of view of violating the rights of a man; and this will disclose effectively the channels of illegal movement of people. It is necessary to use the experience of countries that have already been faced with such problems and taking note of their legalization[9].

In the Southern regions of the Republic of Kazakhstan migration register cards of migrants were implemented because of the possibility of mass uncontrolled migration of Kazakhs from Uzbekistan. It lightened the registration of the foreigners in the country, but simultaneously it might turn to additional source of exactions for corrupted policemen. According to experts, in the near future the volume of illegal migration to Kazakhstan will increase under the influence of the following reasons: pressure from religious extremism, terrorism, drug traffic on all CIS countries but mostly on those countries which are transport corridors; increasing gap between North and South; demographic pressure from China and CAR countries; ethno social and political conflicts in CAR; ecological trans-boundary problems; possible shortfalls in labour and employment markets. According to experts there is need to improve legal provisions relating to illegal migration as it is directly related to the state security. Due to the volume of migration the process of economical and social-demographic destabilization of the society is strengthening. Negative social-economical and political consequences of migration are obvious.

In long-term a serious factor influencing the intensity of migration will be demography. Countries of CAR are on the stage of demographic transfer, which is characterized by high level of birth rate and low death rate. According to the forecasts of UNO, population of CAR countries will increase 1.5 times by 2015. It is obvious that such increase of demographic potential of the region may intensify the problem of unemployment in the next 15–20 years due to insufficient economical development. Uncontrollable mass emigration from the region, first of all labour one, may become the source of social tension[10].

Stabilization of migration processes includes complex social-economical, political-legal and organizational-financial measures; and the development of these measures is impossible without system-defined analysis of departure reasons, economical, political and social-demographic evaluation of its consequences, prediction of emigration flows. In 2000, the majority of Governments of CAR countries approved the Conception of Migration Policy and the Conception of Demographic Policy, and started to develop migration program for 2002–2015; Convention of UNO was signed, which aims against transnational organized crime, but Interdepartmental and Interstate cooperation is not quite intimate yet.

It is necessary to adopt laws on fighting illegal migration, to improve labour legislation, especially in the sphere of the foreign manpower import. It is also necessary to develop institutional base, to strengthen the potential in migration flows control, and to prevent illegal migration (opening new border outposts, strengthening the control over the arriving people). A significant role in illegal migration prevention is played by bilateral and multilateral agreements with Russia, China, Kyrgyzstan, Uzbekistan, Tajikistan, Agreement for Cooperation with CIS countries in illegal migration fighting[11]. In July 2001, issues concerning limitation of illegal migration were viewed as a priority at the meeting of SCO. The International Migration Organization (IMO) coordinates the work on resisting human traffic. Assistance of IMO includes: help in returning to the native land, providing with medical service, rendering specialized psychological help; providing with provisional asylum; rendering judicial services. Also training programs of law machinery in fight and prevention of human traffic was started.

Cooperation with international organizations helps to solve problems of illegal migration, to strengthen the potential of local organizations, to develop consulting help at legislation working out. For instance, IMO realizes the project on women traffic prevention and border control system improvement. Unification of procedures and legislative acts of the countries of EAEU is an important aspect of strengthening the fight against illegal migration. In this connection it is advisable to practice regular exchange of information concerning measures stipulating responsibility of physical and legal entities for assistance to illegal migration. It is necessary to provide cooperation of state-members of EAEU on revealing the channels of illegal migration and suppressing their unlawful activity. It is necessary to arrange deportation of hedge emigrants, to observe strictly migration legislation and registration of migrants with the help of migration cards. National cultural centers and other analogous structures are to verify the number of their immigrants with state migration services, and to bear responsibility for any assistance or concealment of facts of illegal migration.

Illegal migration prevention demands intimate international cooperation. Internal political stability and international image of all CAR countries depend on their position relative to illegal migrants and their transit through the local territories. It is also necessary to define the maximum size of a quota for refugees and to develop provisions for refugees. Some citizens of CAR countries participate in illegal drug production and transit. At this, state bodies are not able to control the situation effectively, especially in those regions with unstable situation (for example, in Tajikistan). Mekhman Gapharly, commentator of "Nezavisimaya Gazeta" ("Independent Newspaper") wrote that "representatives of law machinery, frontier guards, leaders of local administrations, and the majority of population were involved in drug business"[12]. The case is complicated with the fact that drug business is used for political purposes, including destabilization of political situation.

Tajikistan is one of the centers of drug production and transit from Afghanistan to CAR. Poppy and Indian hemp are cultivated there. Conflict in Tajikistan contributes to the growth of drug business. According to the data of the MIA of the Republic of Tajikistan, more than 200 tons of drugs are transported trough the territory of Tajikistan annually, and law machinery seizes only the part of them[13]. Flow of drugs goes to Kyrgyzstan and from there to Kazakhstan, Russia and other states of CIS. In Kyrgyzstan itself there were farms on cultivating poppy for medical needs in Soviet time, 16 per cent of morphine was produced from Kyrgyzstan. Ephedra is also grows in Kyrgyzstan from which ephedrine is produced. Drugs production and transportation from Afghanistan and Iran also takes place in Turkmenistan.

The great base for drugs production, processing and transportation is Kazakhstan, which handles the drug flow from China. According to the data of MIA of RF, 93 per cent of marijuana comes from Kazakhstan to the Russian market, and 85 per cent of hashish and 78 per cent of opium have Kazakhstan origin. Illegal migration and drug business spread distrust among the CAR countries and lead to mutual suspicions and charge of failure of their migration services and law machinery. All this seriously endangers the extension of integration process among the CAR and is a factor for their vulnerability. But it is significant to keep in mind that it would be impossible to stop these negative phenomena without joint efforts.

Notes and References

1. M.B. Olcott and N. Udalova-Zvart, *Drug Trafficking on the Great Silk Road: The Security Environment in Central Asia* of Carnegie's Centre in Moscow, № 2, 2000.
2. "The social-demographic processes in Kazakhstan: 1999–2000, *Sayasat*, № 10–11, 2001, pp. 45–55
3. *Migration in Kazakhstan-present and future,* Materials of the

International Organization for Migration's Seminar. – Astana, January 26–27 2000.

4. E. Sadovskaya, *Migration in Kazakhstan at the beginning of CCI century: basic tendencies and perspectives,* Almaty, 2001.
5. B. Holist, "The organized criminality in Eastern Europe and its influence on the Western World security" Chicago, Illinois: The International criminal Justice Office, 1999, pp. 67–93.
6. O. Khasenov, "The analysis of migrational situation in the sovereign Kazakhstan", *Sayasat*, № 3., 2001, p. 12.
7. G. Tlegenova, N. Shedenova, "The problems of Kazakh women's trafficking: factors of vulnerability and prevention" *Socis,* Almaty, 2000, p. 26.
8. G. Vitkovskaya (ed.), *The world experience of migration policy: retrospective and new tendencies*– Moscow-Almaty: International Organization for Migration, 2004.
9. E. Sadovskaya, "The illegal migration and problems of it's prevention" *Misly*, No. 2, 2002, p. 42.
10. E. Tukumov, "The Kazakhs of Uzbekistan" *Central Asia and the Caucasus*, № 6, 2000, pp. 214–215.
11. *The drug business in the south of Russia: political aspects*, Moscow, 1997.
12. A. Voskresenskii (ed) *East/West: Regional systems and regional problems of the international relations*, Moscow, 2002.
13. *The drug business: Russia's new threat from the East*, Moscow, 1996.

7

Migration and Gender Issue

The Experience of Post-Soviet Tajikistan

Nandini Bhattacharya

Tajikistan is the worst affected state among the successor nations of Central Asia. Throughout most of the final decade of the last century Tajikistan was engulfed in a protracted civil war while the rest of the states in the same zone were on course to consolidate their positions. Although there were a number of similarities in the problems they inherited and the challenges they faced, each of the Central Asian state had their own unique set of issues defined by their geo-strategic position and distinct ethno-cultural makeup. Among the many discernible new traits in the post 1991 transition, one very prominent tendency is towards migration. Although migration is a very common characteristic of all the post-Soviet states, it had a rather unique impact for Tajikistan, given the other particular attributes of this smallest, poorest and the most vulnerable state in Central Asia. Migration emerged as an easy alternative to solve the problem of unemployment for most of the Central Asian states. Tajikistan too had to accept this easy way out for combating hunger and poverty. Remittances from Tajiks settled abroad began to facilitate cash inflow that substantially contributed to improve the general standard of the Tajik economy. The process acted as a safety valve to hold off the extra population without job and food, thereby saving the state from further embarrassment.

But a brief survey of the history of migration in pre-Independence Tajikistan shows a completely different mind-set of the people towards migration. People of Tajikistan displayed very strong inhibition and inertia towards out migration to other economic zones within the USSR. This had adversely affected the Soviet state economy ever since the 70's. This backdrop makes the recent phenomenon of migration worth exploring. It came as an answer to the question of subsistence and survival for a distressed ethno-cultural community, which had to sacrifice their age-old habitat along with their casual and insipid life-style in order to overcome the acute economic crisis. However, migration itself triggered off a broad trajectory of issues of which the most alarming is the question of family and social security related to the changing position of women. Emigrations were mostly single and temporary, which created havoc in the sphere of gender balance. Mostly, the left behinds are women, old people and children that increased the responsibility and challenge for women in general, often creating a kind of emotional vacuum in young women as well.

This paper will attempt to highlight major trends in migration in Tajikistan. It would attempt to explain how migration acted as an easy answer to the present economic crisis, but in the process gave rise to a new set of problems with complex and prolonged effects on the Tajik state and society in transition. One must admit at the very outset, to avoid confusion, that migration too is a common feature of all CIS countries, including Russia herself ever since the collapse of the USSR. Yet, the Tajik experience shows that majority of Tajikistan's emigrant workers seek jobs in Russia and other Central Asian countries. Let us begin with the ILO report on Tajik immigration and its nature.

Migration Trends

Moscow ILO Online states that according to recent ILO report, the Russian Federation is the destination for 85 per cent of Tajikistan's migrant workers. A quarter of the 600,000 Tajik migrants head for Moscow, where they mainly work in the construction industry. It further explains the cause of this out-flow of labour. The monthly average wage in Tajikistan is US$ 12, while a construction worker in Russia can earn US$300.[1] There has been substantial study and analysis of migration as a significant process related to state and economy from various perspectives. One such study mentions, "Tajikistan may be the largest emigrant labour supplier per capita in the world. The best estimates indicate that approximately 600,000 Tajiks, or 18 per cent of the adult population, leave the country every year to seek seasonal work or to work abroad for a couple of years."[2]

The author, Aaron Erlich, of Migration Policy Institute, writing in 2006, in a pre-recession Europe, tried to assess the comparative incentives for migration from Tajikistan to Russia. On the one hand she found poverty, instability and high birth rate as strong push factors for Tajiks to emigrate their home towns or villages while stable economic growth, high wages compared to their native state and labour shortage in Russia acted as necessary pull factor. Almost 80 per cent of the Tajik migrants were absorbed in the Russian construction industries while some remained in Uzbekistan and Kazakhstan. The Tajik migrants mostly concentrate into these areas because they can speak Russian and they cannot manage visa for most other countries. Since Tajikistan is a member of EEC (Eurasian Economic Community), Tajik citizens need not have a visa to visit Russia for ninety days. And this creates a large loop-hole and unregistered labour migration continues side by side with legal emigration records. Since the work permit needed for registering in Russia entail a hazardous process and often based on high bribe, a large number of labours purchase fake permits, and another large number don't even try to have a permit. Thus the ratio between illegal and legal emigrant worker in Russia is 1:9.[3]

The emigrant workers, legal or illegal, are engaged mainly in three types of enterprises, for example, construction industry, open air markets and some shuttle between Russia and homeland to trade small items of commodities. There exist both long and short term labourers working away from Tajikistan, their home visit mostly uncertain and infrequent due to the nature of their jobs and illegal stay. The most visible positive impact of Tajik emigration is the remittance received by their corresponding families. According to IMF report, the net amount of remittance flowing to Tajikistan annually used to range between US$ 400 million and US$ 1 billion in 2006 which amounted to 20–50 per cent of Tajikistan's total GDP. And a major portion of this remittance came from Russia. In order to facilitate the flow of legal remittance and to acknowledge the concern of the migrant workers for the family they left behind, the Tajik government made laws in 2001 to reduce the 30 per cent tax on bank remittance.

It is interesting to note how the Tajik government welcomed this process of human resource outflow ever since the trend began to show up. The laws in the new Tajik constitution are all very liberal for emigration. Thus, the state had a twofold solution at the face of insurmountable economic crisis. The process acted as a safety valve to get rid of the extra population without job and food, thereby saving the state from further embarrassment and allowing them a comparatively better and secure life abroad. Over and above, this emigrant population held a lucrative promise of remittance, which in reality continued to be a substantial proportion of the total income of the state till the world wide recession began to creep in.

However, in reality, seen from a broader perspective, emigration contained a much more complex story with a series of negative impacts in Tajik life and society. Before going into the current development of migration and its impact on the migrants and their families left behind, a brief survey of migration history in pre-Independence Tajikistan is necessary. It is interesting that there was almost complete absence of migration as a regular phenomenon in the Soviet Tajikistan. It was once again a common characteristic of all the Central Asian republics mainly in the rural level. There prevailed a very strong inhibition and inertia towards out migration, to other economic zones within the USSR. This was a matter of high concern for the Soviet analysts as this aversion towards migration to cities within their own state or other neighbouring Soviet republics created a lop-sided distribution of labour supply and management. This had adversely affected the Soviet state economy ever since the 70's. This inertia to move out of the traditional family surrounding affected the economic growth of the region quite adversely for this created an unnecessary burden on rural sector while the urban industrial sector had to borrow workers from European parts of Soviet Union. This created a very complex ethnic equation in the zone. While there was population pressure from within, the general apathy towards migration to urban industrial sectors made the influx of Russian and other skilled workers necessary for industrial activities. The big size of the family and traditional pattern of household deterred the scope or prospect of migration even within the republic, not to speak of going abroad. Arutunian, a well-known Soviet ethnographer observed that there was an inverse relation between migration and family size in rural areas. Analysts of similar category, Susokolov and Ostapenko dealt in detail the prospect of labour mobilization from Central Asia to other parts of the USSR, especially to the rural areas of RSFSR, where there existed an agrarian labour shortage. They called Central Asia, a 'laobur surplus' zone. But the fact that the 'labour surplus' zone was not conducive to the concept of migration was well known fact to the scholars.

They explained the factor which retarded the prospect of mobilization in both psychological and material terms, "The question of why the migration mobility of a number of indigenous populations of the Central Asian and Caucasian republics is so, low is widely considered in the scientific literature. Familiar social and natural surroundings, the moral and economic support of relatives and friends, a reduced likelihood of psychological stresses (a common companion for rural migrants to large cities) all slow resettlement to the city, even within one's own republics."[4] In an article titled.

"Agriculture and Rural Out Migration in Central Asia, 1960–91" Prof. Ajay Patnaik made a systematic analysis to show as to how this peculiar attachment to the roots had affected the economic growth of Soviet Central Asia as a whole. "Its agriculture had the lowest productivity index in the USSR. Over the years a large number of people had become surplus in agriculture and the surplus population had either remained attached to the collective seasonal employment or was engaged in household and private subsidiary activity. Rather than moving to non-agricultural jobs or to urban areas most Central Asia stayed in villages." He further provided specific analysis based on interesting data. "Reports in the mid-1970s showed that nearly a quarter of the able-bodied population in Tajik villages could find jobs in other sectors if normal labour were cut, and no harm would have been done to the rural economy. In 1986, the level of manual labour use in agriculture amounted to over 85 per cent in Tajikistan. Excluding Turkmenia, the rest of the Central Asian Republics used three to five times more manpower per unit of average for the USSR as a whole."[5]

The reasons behind this deliberate refusal to internal migration within the USSR can be answered in terms of ethno-cultural distinctiveness of the region concerned. The institution of family, ethnic ties, rural cultural and environmental attachment that provided a kind of centuries old bond, security and stability which the people were not ready to tamper with even under the revolutionary promises of the so called socialist regime. So, unemployment in a hidden sense prevailed in the form of surplus labour. This backdrop makes the recent phenomenon of migration appear really surprising. It came as an answer to the question of subsistence and survival for a distressed ethno-cultural community, which had to sacrifice their age-old habitat along with their slow life-style in order to overcome the acute economic crisis. As long as the Soviet system survived, this community had a choice between their age-old tradition and the mechanical Soviet alternative. They preferred to stick to their own tradition even at the cost of slow economic growth at that point. But, the post-Soviet era had forced them to stand between tradition and starvation where they had to sacrifice the former to get rid of the latter.

Another research article by Liliya Shvetsova, published just around the break up of the Soviet world had some significant hypothesis on the future trend of migration of the Central Asians. While assessing the general trend of migration of the Post-Soviet communities to the outer world, as an impact of liberalization, she highlighted the very specific context of Central Asia. "Most anxious to emigrate from the post-Soviet states are young people ranging between 20 and 35 years of age, residents of large industrially developed and culturally advanced centers, and representatives of the intellectual, scientific and cultural elite." But the prospect of migration seemed slightly less probable to her at that historic moment although she did not completely rule out the possibility as such. "Residents of middle Asia still living under the structure of semi-feudal relational and territorial ties will be less inclined to leave the motherland. But the inevitable deepening of the economic crisis in the region and the further swelling of the army of unemployed, especially among the young people, could start a rise in migration. It should not be ruled out that local authorities will themselves be attempting to pave the way for emigration or for temporary employment abroad for their compatriots, with the purpose of avoiding a social explosion."[6]

By far this was as a very powerful hypothesis, which has been proved by the events of the succeeding century. But her final intuition about the choice of countries for the majority of the migrants is not yet justified numerically. Considering the prospect of adjustment she felt that the obvious choice of Central Asian emigration would be the Muslim countries, like Turkey, Saudi Arabia, Iran, Pakistan and so on instead of Europe. But as economic pull proves to be more powerful, the migration in bulk is still headed towards Russia. It is true that there is a trend of emigration towards the Muslim countries (mainly Afghanistan), that actually had a clandestine beginning during the late Soviet era. But none of the ruling governments approve or facilitate such developments since these migrations carry dangerous issues like, Islamic fundamentalism, cross border terrorism drug peddling etc, all of which deter the prospect of peace and development. One news report from Dushanbe last year showed a different attitude expressed in Government initiative on migration towards middle-east and other prospective parts of the world: "The Tajik government says it wants to send labour migrants to other countries besides the most common destination, Russia. Tajik Foreign Minister Hamrohkhon Zarifi told RFE/RL's Tajik Service that the government is discussing ways to send Tajik citizens to South Korea, Qatar, Yemen, and other Arab countries for work. Labour and Social Affairs Minister Shukurjon Zuhurov said in Dushanbe that Tajikistan is capable of sending 20,000 to 50,000 workers to the Middle East and South Korea every year. More than 800,000 Tajiks go to Russia each year seeking work."[7] This was probably an after thought for recession caused a sudden fall in the flow of migration towards Russia.

A working paper on Migration and Poverty Reduction in Tajikistan summarized the pros and cones of the migration process and the Government response to it. The authors overwhelmingly stressed the benefits of migration and how it had acted as a blessing for the jobless population and dwindling national economy: "In the context of Tajikistan's domestic economy, migration has acted as a clear 'shock absorber' that has relieved societal tension in an economy undergoing transition. In the wider context, migration from Tajikistan is the natural response of a poor landlocked country to the pressures of globalisation. Overall, labour migration has had an observable stabilising and developmental impact, especially on poverty reduction and economic growth."[8] But this was an incomplete depiction of the process.

Once migration began as a way out in bulk it had voluminous impact on the family of the emigrants who were left behind and changed the demographic profile of Tajikistan. The nature of emigrations being single and temporary it created havoc in the sphere of gender balance. Majority of the able bodied men left for job with a promise of remittance but that process in large scale had created an unusual social imbalance. Tajikistan, especially rural Tajikistan lacks able-bodied young men. Mostly, the left behinds are women, old people and children, that increased the responsibility and challenge for women in general. And social life showed a kind of lop-sidedness, for young women this created a kind of emotional vacuum as well. Thus migration created a psycho-social trauma for the Tajik women and increased the challenge of day to day existence many fold.

Tajik Scenario

The Interior Ministry claims that 500,000 Tajiks worked in Russia in 2007 by official estimates and more than a million by unofficial. Usmanova admitted the lack of an efficient system of immigration control in the republic and complained that Tajikistan couldn't afford it." So she continues to wonder, "That nearly 1 million Tajiks seek employment abroad every year is a sure sign of there being something wrong with the Tajik state itself." And answers her own question from a very basic, practical point of view, "Average monthly pay in Tajikistan is $36, minimum $3.75. Immigration is not going to dwindle therefore, and legalization of everyone eager to seek employment abroad is a sheer impossibility" She ends up her article depicting the prevailing mood of desolation and despair and gave a sharp alarm to rouse the conscience of the Tajik state authorities.

> Lots of Tajik boys barely out of school pack up and leave for Russia nowadays. This exodus will only continue and whether or not they ever decide to come back is not a foregone conclusion at all. It should alert the authorities. The young, healthy, and strong leave the country, and national genetic resources deserve better than that. Either Tajikistan begins to take the problem seriously and undertakes to do something about impoverishment, or it will certainly find itself in trouble soon."[9] It seems Tajikistan is catapulted into a vicious cycle of poverty and migration that caused them sacrifice the rhythm of simple normal family life. In fact, scholars working on migration repeatedly questioned the future of

> family and society in case such uncertain tenure of immigration went on: "Temporary immigration is feared to produce an ethnic underclass where we see the extremes of a process of increasing job uncertainty, which affects this category of population particularly hard and leads to serious breakdown in its social cohesion. This situation raises question: Is immigration weakening the links that hold families and communities together?[10]

An ADB report of a village called Tojjikon emphasized the crisis in grass root level. The article begins by the depiction of the emptiness, the vacuum that the village men had left behind. "It is late afternoon, yet the main street of this village is eerily quiet. It takes a while to realize what is missing: groups of men standing or sitting around, smoking, and gossiping." The article mentioned an interview with one such individual family that actually represented the plight of the entire village community. On this street, we have 22 families, yet only three male heads of family, including myself, are here," says Dr. Zabiyuvlo Teshaev, the village doctor. The other men are away most of the time. "Dilafruz, the doctor's 22-year-old daughter, has been married to Khayol, 24, for 5 years. They have one child. But she sees her husband for only a few months each year. Around February, he makes the long journey to Russia to work on construction sites and does not return till around October. Most migrant men like Khayol work in the building industry but others find employment in factories and plants. Dilafruz has her own house, but is lonely without her husband and spends a lot of time in the home of her father and sisters. 'Of course, it is hard bringing up my baby alone, and I miss my husband,' she says."[11]

This lonely doctor and his lonelier young daughter who leads a married life without the togetherness and sharing, and who brings up her child all alone amidst poverty, uncertainty and boredom represent the fate of the milieu in almost all villages. As the article further observed, "There are few options for the men who stay behind. In the Vorukh area, which includes Tojicon, a UNDP official says some 7,000–8,000 men leave to work abroad; of those who remain, 3,800 work on collective farms, 600 are employed in schools, 40 in the hospital, and 20 in administration. The wages for those who stay are very low. For example, Dr. Teshaev, a graduate of Dushanbe Medical Institute and one of the most educated villagers, treats patients for free at his home and receives the standard government salary of $7 a month. He survives by supplementing his income from selling apricots grown in his garden.

The migrants' absence also has an impact on those they leave behind. Women lead a conservative life in these rural areas. Girls are expected to marry at 14, and their lives revolve around the home. Children have to grow up without fathers. The lack of a male role model and paternal discipline can have a negative impact upon youth in villages where dropout rate from schools is already high and social centers and jobs are lacking. A UNDP official says frustration and boredom create conditions for disorderly behavior, such as fighting, drunkenness, and petty crime."[12] An echo of the same voice of despair is reflected in the article of Rachel Ellison. She chanced upon meeting a number of young women whose husbands stayed away for job. "One of our journalism trainees, Bichalicha, was often late for our seminar. I stopped her on the stairs to ask if there was a problem. "My husband is away and I have two jobs as well as the children to look after," she replied, catching her breath. "My husband hasn't sent any money from Russia. I don't even know when I'll next see him." You would never know that this beautiful, educated woman, in her traditional voluminous velvet, ankle-length dress of green and gold, was struggling to hold it all together. Bichalicha smiled warmly and added: "I just try to keep going for the children's sake." I did not dare ask what she would do if her husband did not return. Of the husbands who do return from Russia, plenty bring a suitcase packed full of roubles, but an increasing number of men are also carrying HIV. Most Tajik women have little idea about HIV/ AIDS."[13]

An ADB report on the condition of Tajik women in post-Soviet era emphasized the issue of migration along with others as decisive factors that determined the economic plight of women along with psycho-social stress. The female headed households, FHH as they are referred in the report faced much larger challenges compared to the MHH, the male headed households as came out from the extensive survey and analysis. "Female headed households are likely to face particular problems The Civil war created approximately 25,000 female headed households predominantly in Khalton and Garm. Some women lost their husbands during the civil war. Others lost their husbands to emigration. A few of the latter group abandoned their families and created new families. In all of these cases, the women became the head of the household. According to 'Save the Children 1998 Socio-Economic Survey of Household, Farms and Bazaars', FHHs have less access to land, irrigation and livestock. They are also less food secure but receive more humanitarian assistance. Even with this assistance, their monthly income is less than male headed households."[14]

Thus, women received the steering wheel to conduct the family by default and neither their society, nor their state were fully prepared to face this unwarranted transformation. Although under the Soviet regime some of the brutal practices against women had been largely eradicated and an apparent equality of rights had been propagated, in terms of real power distribution and sharing entire Central Asia continued to be overwhelmingly patriarchal where women hardly performed any decision making role. Whether in household or in the work force her role in subordination to the male counterparts went on unabated. After the independence, a number of women's rights had to be thought over. The most remarkable one is her land right. But even with the technical rights been achieved, women keep on facing problems in realizing them for the social taboo attached to the image of women as such. But the absence of men created a peculiar paradox where women had to perform the tasks of physical work, economic responsibility and family or house hold decisions by far delineated for men while her centuries old mind set of subordination and image of a protection seeker deters her from enjoying the power that entailed with this challenge. Nor the society along with its remnant male population allows women to feel confident of this changed position. Of course, given the atmosphere of poverty and other insecurities women headed households are actually sites of female vulnerability rather than their empowerment. The social set up remaining overwhelmingly traditional, some stereo-typical image of a woman still continues to be appreciated in the inter-personal family ties and the social and professional life reflects extension of the same structure. Muriel Atkin in a book review stated the expected image of each family member in a Tajik household: Both sexes have clearly defined roles to play at various stages of their lives: unfailingly obedient children, the male head of household, the fearsome mother-in-law, and the exploited daughter in law."[15] Atkin further highlighted the grim condition of women as found from survey that, "Opportunities for careers outside the home would have been discouraged as improper for a Tajik woman in Soviet times and are even less of an option now, with the economy in bad shape and educational opportunities reduced. The current economic hardships have worsened relations between husbands and wives, as men vent their frustration on their wives in the form of abuse or leave the family for jobs in Russia, where they may form new relationships."[16]

The ADB report also highlighted this fact of discrimination in real terms towards women in land rights as even their capabilities to conduct agricultural work had often been questioned. Although there is extensive use of female labour in cultivation yet, in a woman headed house hold her land right is questioned for the lack of 'man power'! As a result, the power vacuum created in gender relation in Tajikistan is being addressed from various dubious angles by many women who could neither carry on the hardship and suffering to have both ends meet and continue the lone battle of establishing her own rights as against the challenges thrown by the traditional power hierarchy. The condition became even more complex with the crumpling of the patriarchal structure in reality, which used to provide women some kind of social security and stability and defined her role and performance in family, society and economy. In the changed situation, the old form become redundant yet, suitable alternative models could not be worked out. An article by a Tajik sociologist with gender specialization very pointedly highlighted this transition in husband-wife relationship. It addressed the role-crisis experienced by the male members of the Tajik society, who according to the scholar ought to change their mind set but regretted that, "The changes in their lives are essential, but not recognized by the society yet." She further elaborated her observation on this shifting balance. "Men's traditional role in Tajikistan is that of a bread-earner and an owner. But today's material difficulties lessened men's power in the family. Sometimes men still demonstrate it, but most of the time only symbolically. The situation leads to conflicts in the family, as the husbands, who are unable to bring enough income to the family express their aggression in the family. The aggression leads to the increase of such problems ass drug addiction, alcoholism, criminality."[17] The form of society in its changing momentum reflects a lack of balance in gender relations. The involvement in productive economy and direct responsibility of running the family or household did not enable women to enjoy real power. Nor the failure of men's economic responsibility in family limited their age old habit of domination. Even in case of absence of male domination within immediate family structure, the society and even the representatives of the state acted as extended family and controlled the conduct of such women. This is mostly reflected in the process of implementing land tenure and agriculture.

A project report of UNIFEM on the "Needs assessment of Rural Women on Land Tenure In Tajikistan" provides a detailed survey of the laws on land and their implementation along with their impact on women of Tajikistan. Interestingly, land right was a very new phenomenon of post-Soviet Central Asia as Soviet system till its end carried on agriculture through collective farms. As a result, individual land right had been one of the crucial reforms that was needed to be launched immediately after independence. According to the report, "Land reform began with the Law "On Dehqan Farms" in 1992, which gave each citizen the right to a dehqan farm, which the head of the farm holds in life-long inheritable tenure rights, to be created from the local rayon administration's reserve land fund. The law called for the breakup of the collective farms, kolkhozes, and state farms, goskhoz, into individual land shares for their members."[18] The survey work had revealed the common experience of absence in male members and the various difficult outcomes of this phenomenon for the women who run the house:

"Of the 34 interviewed households, the husbands in 12 (33%) were absent. The reasons given for the absence of the men were the poor economic conditions that have led many male heads of household to migrate to find work. Many of the men have gone to Russia. Some come home once a year, others do not return for 5–6 years. If they do come home once a year, it is usually at end of fall, to stay for about for two months. In the studied Urmetan Village of Urmetan Jamoat, Aini District, some husbands had never been back since they left, and some have never had any contact with their families. Another important reason for the absence of men is the Civil Conflict (1992–97), which created a remarkable number of widows. In the household interviews, 79 per cent of those interviewed said that the number of female-headed households has increased and continues to increase".[19]

Another interesting finding of the survey is the fact that in spite of the introduction of the individual ownership of the lands, the production continues in the collective farm mode in the operative level. Experiences of survey in the villages like Karchin, Sahgirdasht, Nishusp etc. many such instances have been traced where dehqan lands are cultivated in the *goskhoz* form. And this had an adverse impact on women's empowerment and real right over her tenure, for in collective form of farming, she is invariably subordinate to some or other male leadership, even if she is the head of her own house-hold. "The village leaders interviewed indicated that in the *kolkhoz* and *goskhoz*, men did leading and commanding work. They are still seen as the most important part of the labor force, going abroad to work. In the *kolkhoz* and *goskhoz*, the village leaders estimated that 60 per cent of the work was done by men and 40 per cent by women. But in recent years, they said, men's work in collective agriculture has decreased because payments are low and uncertain, and more men have left the villages to find jobs elsewhere.

However, this shift in balance did not bring any good fortune for women. For, when women work as paid labour, they are paid less than men. Although the same report iterated that in some villages, the village leaders even indicated that women had done more than 80 per cent of the agricultural work.[20] Even if a woman had her land to cultivate on her own there are problems. One survey on Gorno Badakhshan reported, "A young widowed woman (in her 30s) reported particular difficulties in recruiting male labour to help with ploughing and preparing the land. She confided that villagers 'gossiped' and made her feel that she was trying to 'get a man' when she asked for male help with farming. A widow in Darwaz who makes a living by selling tomatoes wept when she described how some people treated her because she was a street vendor."[21] Thus women developed their own set of grievances which they confided in their interviews with the survey workers. Not that each had experienced all the problems, but they mostly share a common sense of insecurity, a common pressure of economic responsibility and over and above, a common lack of recognition by the society.

Asked about their concerns and needs, the women in the focus groups said that:

- While they do most of the agricultural work, they are unhappy that they must always do it under men's leadership.
- They felt terribly burdened by needing to do both women and men's work and, when their men were absent, the men's work.
- They resented the hard and almost unpaid labour in the collective farms.
- They feared the extreme poverty and unemployment during winters.
- They regretted their husbands' unemployment and migration to find jobs.
- They were concerned about lack of funding to start businesses, low wages, what they saw as a high land tax rate, poor health care, poor education and especially poor education for girls and lack of childcare.

- They were aware that they lacked knowledge of their rights, and said they needed training."[22]

Since, independence brought along such series of hardships, uncertainty and dislocation in the socio-economic level there developed a natural comparison with the previous Soviet era. Opinions varied as the surveys reflect. Some exalted the freedom of individual choice in dehqan faming, where the owner of the land had no other obligation but paying taxes. A number of dehqan holders, on the contrary stated that they had been better off in the former Soviet system that provided better education and health services. One respondent lamented, "they had freedom to have land and market crops; and they also had the freedom to be poor."[23]

Women in Aini District seemed to particularly miss the collective services, and complained of their loss of services: "In the prime kolkhoz times, wages were paid and paid on time. Kindergartens were available to children and women. Free food was provided to kolkhoz members. Stores offered all types of goods at low prices, and one could afford them. Women's everyday expenses and living requirements were provided by the collective farms. Now, they complained, "our lives and necessities are controlled by our men. We don't have kindergartens, we are not paid, and we work only for some tobacco in the collective farm. Tobacco used to be a source of income, but now there is not demand for it."

Kanji's survey showed how the economic retrogression is associated with both physical and psychological stress for men and women. According to some women, men had a much easier life in Soviet era and became lazy and spent time in drinking and socializing. "Now men work much harder on land and this has been the most difficult adjustment they had to make. Both women and men are carrying out manual work that was previously performed by tractors, harvesters and milling machines."[24] The lop sided gender balance as it is found, created a tremendous stress on the woman in their everyday struggle for existence. Attitude towards single women, whether widowed, or left by the husbands remain precarious in a traditional mindset. A strangle demand to legalize polygamy had been raised by women themselves in order to have a quick solution. This obviously would strengthen the patriarchal repression manifold and take them back to medieval household despotism that they could transcend to a large extent through the Soviet intervention. Thus, women, captive of patriarchal order in their body and mind demanded to turn the history back instead of moving forward transcending the need of male support or guardianship.

However, the government has taken a rational stand regarding polygamy. They vehemently refute the prospect of allowing polygamy any legal foothold in the society in transition. One such senior government official Latofat Nasriddinova, head of the committee for women's affairs and family, told IWPR (Institute for War and Peace Reporting) that the rights of women would be infringed even more if polygamy was legalized. Gulafzo Savriddinova, vice-speaker of the lower house of the Tajik parliament, is split on the issue. She believes that the law should punish polygamists, but sympathises with their wives and thinks that their rights should be protected in some way. But there are other representatives who showed inclinations in support of legalizing the practice of polygamy. Mukhiddin Kabiri, deputy head of the Islamic Revival Party of Tajikistan, told IWPR, "The current political leadership of Tajikistan is not yet ready to legalize polygamy in our country, although this phenomenon has become a reality,"

A group of Tajik women – mostly the wives of polygamous husbands – recently wrote a letter to the country's parliament, asking for their status to be legitimized.[25] There are end less debates arising out of the fate and future of the second wives and their children. For example while Nargiz Zakirova, a local journalist in Tajikistan, demanded there is an increasing need to legalize the practice to protect the rights of women and children in polygamous families for in second or third marriages children are deprived of all rights just as their mothers. She observed, "In order to identify legal fatherhood, there are many documents that should be collected. Some men deny their paternity, and not all men give their names to children from second or third wives."[26]

But Layli Babaeva, a deputy in the Tajik parliament, is against the introduction of legal polygamy. She expressed in clear terms, "Nobody will introduce such a law in our legislation, first of all. Secondly, our current laws do not deprive children from second or third marriages their rights. According to our laws, if you prove that you are cohabitating with a man, then regardless of whether you have a stamp or not [registration of a marriage], a man has to support and help that woman. Their children have the same rights like ones born out of wedlock."[27] But even the Islamic authorities are not always happy about this trend towards polygamy and sometimes criticize this trend as a nothing but carnal desire on part of the men concerned. The former mufti of Central Asia, Muhammad Sodiq Muhammad Yusuf, says – "If you look at the attitude of these newly polygamous men toward Islam, then you'll see that most of them do not practice any Islamic rules but rush into polygamy and justify it as legal from an Islamic point of view. Mainly, they are acting to satisfy their sexual desires."[28]

Another cause for alarm is the increasing numbers involved in human trafficking. There are news articles from the very onset of the present century as to how this process of trafficking worked. One such news article stated, "The IOM (International Organization for Migration) has released a survey that estimates some 1,000 women from Tajikistan fell victim to traffickers last year, and that most of them, as has been the case for women from other Central Asian republics, ended up in sexual or domestic servitude, mainly in the Gulf states and Russia."[29] The issue remained equally alarming for the countries in Central Asia, including Tajikistan after one decade of awareness and struggle with the painful journey towards economic sustenance. It has been observed in an online news track, that at least one thousand Tajik women are trafficked annually and of them majority are sent to Saudi Arabia. Recently, Tajik state had passed a law to prevent forced trafficking." Tajik women trafficked to Arab countries are sent there through other countries. Deputy Director of Dushanbe Airport Aziz Ibrogimov said it is forbidden for women who are under 30 to fly to Arab countries unaccompanied. "That measure was taken to prevent the trade of women that is already the third most profitable form of criminal trade in the world, following only weapons and drug trafficking," Ibrogimov said. The criminals luring women into sexual slavery get them out of the country through Moscow, Bishkek and Almaty, he said."[30]

But another Tajik correspondent on the contrary claimed "Not All Tajik Women Go Abroad to Work as Prostitutes", some of them also do normal jobs she stated. But she too admitted that scope of ordinary jobs and business must be created to prevent this kind of degeneration and exploitation of the Tajik women.[31]

There are more and more references of Tajik women seeking job through migration in the recent years. Another report of RFE/RL mentioned the marked increase in the number of women job seekers abroad. "Within the overall phenomenon of Tajik labor migration, new tendencies are seeming to emerge. Mukarrama Burhonova, who works at an IOM information center in Tajikistan, told RFE/RL's Tajik Service on 14 June that 40 percent of the 1,500 potential migrant workers who visited the center over the past two months were women. Six months ago, she said, the center received only 10–20 women a month. Now they number from 200 to 500. "The number of male migrant workers is very large, but women are not far behind, and women are more insistent about gathering information than men," Burhonova said. Nozanin Huseynova, a woman from Dushanbe with eight children, came to the IOM center to find out what she could before departing for Russia for the first time. Beset by poverty, Huseynova said that going to Russia to work is the best solution to the problem of supporting her family and paying for her children's education. "Six of my children are studying in middle school or college. My husband is unemployed. My children don't have a chance to continue their education because middle school costs money, college costs money, and we can't afford it," Huseynova said. "The country's leaders don't spend a lot of time thinking about things like this, do they? But I see going to Russia as the way out of these everyday problems."[32]

However, not that all emigrations from Tajikistan fall into the same category. Although in this paper the emphasis was mainly on emigration of rural Tajikistan to Russia as unskilled labourers, since this trend had created a havoc in the social security of the village society and brought untold hardship to the life of women they had left behind. Yet, this should not blur the achievements of those Tajik youths who, taking advantage of the brighter side of globalization migrated out of their motherland to further study or enhance their professional skills. There are quite a number of young Tajik students studying abroad with prestigious scholarships. Many of them came back after successful completion of their study and took up responsible jobs in Tajikistan itself. And there are also some, who took up jobs abroad but are strongly in touch with the motherland. This may open up a new window towards the understanding of the Tajik society and its future trends as a whole. They create a very small yet distinguished community of Tajiks representing their land and culture to the world. There are young women belonging to this category who aspire for true educational and cultural development. This paper does not focus on their achievements in details, but it acknowledges their presence as a positive factor in the transition process of this country. But their number is negligible compared to their unfortunate sisters who still face the unforeseen miseries for no faults of their own. The distancing of marital relationship is growing in various directions and leading to break ups in unprecedented manner.

Conclusions

The Tajik social security is endangered at different levels and in various degrees as a part of common inheritance of all the CIS countries. Migration and the complexities arising out of it is an experience shared by almost all the post-Soviet nationalities including the Great Russian people. Russia as a new federation is undergoing innumerable economic crises and out-migration to more prosperous global territories continues to be a regular feature. But the fact that the Tajiks seek asylum to Russia for food and shelter speaks volume about the magnitude of their poverty and misery. Rebuilding the new nation remains a grave challenge for each of these countries, especially with the silent pressure to transcend the shadow of the Soviet experience – an experiment which collapsed headlong. Each of the members of the post-Soviet world carries the embarrassment of that debacle. But, through each day's struggle for survival they realise their inherent bonding to a system that though not perfect, provided stability and basic security in everyday life of the ordinary people.

In a personal interview, a very senior Professor named Kh. Umarov, who is a specialist in Economics, strongly upheld the Soviet period as a Golden Age compared to the downtrodden situation of contemporary Tajikistan.[33] Similarly, a very young and vibrant Tajik emigrant student Gulshan Zuguratnikova iterated the same phrase of 'golden age' for the lost socialist era.[34] An echo of the same view is iterated in Nazneen Kanji's survey – "People in Tajikistan look upon the Soviet period as a golden era. All the women we talked to, without exception, said that life was much better in Soviet times. They talked about their higher material standard of living, described the low prices and variety of food available in the shops. Free health care and education were important and they claimed to have enough money to satisfy their basic needs."[35]

The phase of transition is difficult for all but it is most probably the most punishing for Tajikistan, given all the socio-economic constraints it faces. Migration as a quick answer to the pressing question of poverty had some apparent benefits. But in the long run this has further complicated the social scenario and brought new challenges to the concept of family. Women, who are mostly at the receiving end of the process, are the victims of uncertainty and desertion. The solutions sought after, as yet are neither very reassuring. The role of migration as a 'social shock absorber' against poverty thus seems to have boomerang into a number of deeper shocks that the Tajik society is destined to bear in future. For social sustenance and temporary economic relief, migration was a quick solution; but like any quick remedy it has too many harmful side effects that endanger the social foundations of the Tajik society in the long run.

Notes and References

1. Organizing out of poverty: the role of trade unions [Feature articles] www.ilo.org/global/About_the_ILO/.../index.html
2. Aaron Erlich, *Tajikistan: From Refugee Sender to Labor Exporter*, July 2006. Migration Policy Institute.
3. *Ibid.*
4. Nandini Bhattacharya, *Dueling Isms: Soviet and Regional Identity in Central Asia*, Shipra Publications, Delhi, 2008, pp. 188–189.
5. Ajay Patnaik, 'Agriculture and Rural Out-Migration in Central Asia, 1960–91', *Europe Asia Studies*, Vol. 47, No. 1 (1995), p. 147.

6. Lilia Shevtsova, 'Post-Soviet Emigration Today and Tomorrow', *International Migration Review,* Vol. 26, No. 2, Special Issue, The New Europe & International Migration, Summer, 1992, p. 245.
7. Tajikistan To Expand Labor Migration To Mideast, Asia January 23, 2009, DUSHANBE http://www.rferl.org/content/Tajikistan_To_Expand_Labor_Migration_To_Mideast_Asia/1373845.html
8. Larissa Jones, Richard Black, Ronald Skeldon, *Globalization and Poverty, Development* Research Centre on Migration, Institute of Migration Studies, Sussex Centre for Migration Research, February, 2007, p. 25
9. Olga Senchuk, Army of labor immigrants from Tajikistan is swelling in numbers, and nothing can stop the process, Central Asia News, Ferghana.ru information agency, 26.12.2007, 12:13.
10. Najam Abbas, Analysing Tajikistan's Labour Market Dynamics: 1997–2007, *Contemporary Central Asia*, Vol. XI, No. 3, p. 41.
11. Gill Ian, (igill@adb.org) Villages without Men, ADB Review [October 2005]
12. *Ibid*
13. *Ibid*
14. ADB *op. cit.*, p. 87.
15. Muriel Atkin, *Book Review* of Colette Harries, Control And Subversion: Gender Relations in Tajikistan, London: Pluto Press, 2004., *Slavic Review*, Vol. 65, No. 3, Autumn, 2006, p. 595.
16. *Ibid.* p. 596.
17. Sofia Kasymova, 'Role Crisis, Do The Men of Tajikistan Change?' *CaucAsia*, International Coalition of Gender Journalists, 6th June, 2005, p. 4.
18. Li Zongmin, *Needs Assessment of Rural Women on Land Tenure Rights in Tajikistan,* UNIFEM, p. 3.
19. *Ibid*, pp. 6–7.
20. *Ibid*, pp. 7–8.
21. Kanji, *op.cit.* p. 144.
22. UNIFEM, *op. cit.* p. 10–11.
23. Kanji, Nazneen, *op. cit.* p. 141.
24. *Ibid.* P. 146.
25. Zamira Eshanova, 'Central Asia: Increase In Polygamy Attributed To Economic Hardship, Return To Tradition', A EurasiaNet Partner Post from RFE/RL, 10/20/02.
26. Nargis Zakirova, *Tajikistan*, RCA No. 151, 4 Oct 2002.

27. Zamira Eshanova, *op. cit.*
28. *Ibid.*
29. Gustavo Capidevila, 'Globalization Leads to Slavery', *Asia Times Online,* Aug 23, 2001.
30. Nijina Sharipova, "Tajik Women Trafficked to Arab Countries through Neighbouring States', *Central Asia Online*, 8.6.09.
31. O. Bobonazarova "Not All Tajik Women Go Abroad to Work as Prostitutes" Dushanbe, September 21 – "Avesta" (Pirnazarov N.) – *Submitted by Nigor Khaitova, National VAW Monitor for Tajikistan.2 /4/2005 9:45 AM 2.*
32. Daniel Kimmage, Tajikistan: Migrant Dangers and Dreams, *RFE/ RL,* August, 22, 2005.
33. Khojamakhmad Umarov, Professor, Head of macro-economic studies department, Institute of Economic Researches, Ministry of Economic Development and Trade, Dushanbe.
34. Z. Gulshan, (from Dushanbe), An M. Phil. Student under ICCR scholarship in Jawaharlal Nehru University, New Delhi.
35. Kanji, *op. cit.* p. 141.

8

Kazakhstan: The Challenges of Ethnic Repatriation and Labour Migration

Bhavna Dave

An important feature of the transition paradigm is the establishment of an open, democratic, ethnically and culturally inclusive state framework. This entails a shift from the prevalent state-regulated ethnonational sphere, characterised by an institutionalised distinction between the 'titular' and 'nontitular' ethnic groups, to one which is geared toward the establishment of an inclusive multiethnic or civic model of nationhood and citizenship.

Kazakhstan, which was hailed during Soviet years as a 'microcosm of a hundred nationalities and languages', attempted to steer its transition to a capitalist, market-oriented economy to bolster a vision of a 'national state' (*natsional'noe gosudarstvo*) during the first decade of its independence. By seeing the state as the symbol of the titular nation, this vision entrusted it with the responsibility of alleviating the demographic, political and cultural marginalisation of the titular nationality by enacting remedial action.[1]

A crucial element in the pursuit of its nationalising vision was the policy launched in 1992 of seeking the return of ethnic Kazakh diaspora (referred to as the *oralman*) settled abroad.

It portrayed the diaspora Kazakhs, concentrated in the adjacent states (China and Mongolia had the largest concentration followed by Afghanistan, Pakistan, Iraq, Turkey as well as in former Soviet territories) as natural citizens of the new state and as potentially more loyal than the non-titular groups residing in Kazakhstan then. Certain members of the ruling Kazakh elite saw the solidarity emanating from a common or 'primordial' trait of ethnicity and kinship as more salient than the purported 'patriotism' of many Russian-speakers towards the Kazakhstani state. In this regard, the repatriation of the co-ethnics was seen as a vital solution to Kazakhstan's demographic anxieties.

The foremost concern for Kazakhstan's ruling elites was to achieve a majority status of the titular Kazakhs and to secure control over the Russian-dominated northern and eastern territories bordering the Russian Federation. In response to the notion of a 'Greater Russia' advocated by key Russian political and cultural figures in these regions and in Russia, the Nazarbaev leadership perceived the preponderant Russian share in its border regions as constituting an imminent irredentist and separatist threat to the nascent sovereignty of their new state. The securitization of the ethnic issue by the Nazarbaev regime, which averred that the dominance of Russians in the border regions constituted a threat to security in the Central Asian region as a whole, played a vital role in broadening the OSCE framework to include the five states of Central Asia and in facilitating an active engagement of the OSCE High Commission on National Minorities in Kazakhstan during the 1990s.[2] Kazakhstan's nation building efforts in its first decade of transition were thus geared towards the establishment of a nationalising or a national state. At the same time, in response to a variety of national, regional and international pressures, its ruling authorities punctuated these nationalising policies with numerous symbolic and declaratory pledges to preserve its multiethnic Soviet legacy and offered ideologised formulations aimed at forging an inclusive civic ('Kazakhstani') identity.

The challenges faced by Kazakhstan's ruling establishment since 2001 are radically different and necessitate a different set of policies and responses. Its rapid economic upturn from 2001 onward has led to an influx of labour migrants, mainly from the CIS states and predominantly from neighbouring Kyrgyzstan, Uzbekistan and Tajikistan. Lacking suitable employment prospects at home, these migrants began fulfilling the need for skilled and unskilled labour generated by Kazakhstan's economy, which registered an 8–10 per cent growth in its GDP during the years 2001–2007. The migrants are employed largely in the construction and service sectors in Almaty and Astana, and in the agricultural sector in rural areas with many working as seasonal workers. They are largely undocumented and unregistered, and therefore without a legal status. Their number in Kazakhstan was estimated to be between 500,000 to a million in 2008. Though the continuing financial crisis since then has lowered the inflow of new migrants, it has not led to a significant departure of the existing migrants. Kazakhstan's demographic and economic reality on the one hand and regional and global migration trends on the other suggest that migrant labour is becoming an integral component of its economy and social sector.

This article depicts the tensions and incongruities in

Kazakhstan's efforts to establish a national state by securing the return of Kazakh diaspora to enhance the numerical status of titular Kazakhs on the one hand and the demand for labour force generated by its expanding economy on the other which can only be met by foreign migrants. Notwithstanding its small demographic base (its population in 1999 census was 14.8 million) and an anticipated labour deficit, Kazakhstan lacks an effective mechanism of legally recruiting foreign migrant labour. Its migration policy is defined entirely by the goal of securing the repatriation of the *oralman*, who in the 1990s were also seen as a solution to its demographic deficit and providing the much needed labour force. There is a broad agreement that the policy of ethnic repatriation has failed to achieve the desired objectives of establishing a national state with a cohesive Kazakh identity or of preparing the necessary labour force to meet the demands of its growing economy. Driven by a short-term economic logic, Kazakhstan's ruling authorities see migration as fulfilling temporary labour needs, rather than as an inevitable corollary of the country's demographic deficit and geographic location in Eurasia. The pursuit of the ethnonational vision is a crucial stumbling block in establishing a legal and normative framework that allows the migrants to work legally and become eligible for settlement.

The first section of this article discusses the specific demographic and nation-building challenges faced by Kazakhstan during its first decade of transition which set the context for launching the policy of seeking a return of the Kazakh diaspora. It situates these repatriation measures in the broad framework of securitization that guided the state's treatment of its nontitular groups. The next section identifies the complexities and challenges that the government has encountered in integrating the returnees or *oralman* into the nationalizing state framework. The last section details the resistance to formulating an appropriate migration policy that will allow Kazakhstan to regulate and legalize the growing influx of transnational labour migrants.

Demographic and Nation-building Challenges in the 1990s

As indicated above, Kazakhstan did not formulate a clear demographic or migration policy that could adequately address the challenges emanating from its transition from a Soviet era settler colony to a sovereign nation, endowed with an enormous anomaly between its territorial size and population base. As the ninth largest country the world, straddling the vast Eurasian landmass between Russia and China, it had a population of only 16.4 million.

An overriding concern for the newly independent Kazakhstani state was to secure a majority status for the titular Kazakhs, who then composed a bare plurality, numbering about 42 per cent of the population. Russians constituted 40 per cent though the Russian-speaking groups together formed a majority. In this light, an emotional call for return of the Kazakh diaspora, referred to as *oralman* (the term connotes a clan that has been separated from its tribe) to its historical homeland was issued at the First All-Kazakh *kurultai* (Congress) in October 1992. Many Kazakhs had fled to the neighbouring countries of Mongolia, China, Afghanistan, Iraq, Turkey, and beyond during the forced settlement of nomads under Stalin and several others followed in subsequent years to unite with their kin abroad.[3] The key consideration was to unify the Kazakhs under one roof to forge a stronger, sustainable Kazakh nation founded on the principle of 'self-determination of the Kazakh people' on its ancestral lands. The co-ethnics were portrayed as harbingers of a pristine Kazakh culture and language that had been contaminated under the induced campaigns of internationalism and Russification.

A number of patriotic-minded scholars projected a rapid rise in the Kazakh share in the population by assuming that a vast proportion of the Kazakh diaspora, whose number was estimated to range from some 4 to 7 million, would return of their newly-sovereign ethnic homeland. There are no reliable data on how many ethnic Kazakhs live outside of Kazakhstan; how many of these are *oralman*, i.e., those separated from their kin due to the Stalinist collectivization policies that put a brutal end to the nomadic economy and forced many Kazakh to flee the country in order to survive; and how many of them migrated for other reasons and not directly in response to persecution. Nor is there any credible information on how many Kazakhs living abroad desire a return to Kazakhstan.

Kazakh demographers in early 1990s surmised that about one fourth to a third of all Kazakhs lived outside of Kazakhstan. The largest concentration of Kazakhs was in the Xinjiang Autonomous Region in China (where Kazakhs currently form 1.5 million), followed by about 800,000 to a million in Russia, about 650,000 in Uzbekistan, 300,000 in Mongolia, and others in Turkey, Afghanistan, and Iran. Makash Tatimov, Kazakhstan's leading demographer in the early 1990s and an advisor on migration and nationalities policies then, grossly inflated the number of Kazakhs in

Kazakhstan and abroad and also exaggerated the natural increase in their numbers. His projections that the total number of Kazakhs in the world will reach about 15 million by the year 2025 and that an overwhelming proportion of these would live in Kazakhstan have proved to be a gross exaggeration.[4] The number of Kazakhs in Kazakhstan is currently about 8.5 million, which includes about 750,000 to 850,000 who have settled in Kazakhstan since 1992.[5] The number of Kazakh diaspora living abroad in the 1990s was estimated to be about 4.1 million, still an inflated estimate.[6]

Repatriation, Non-titular Emigration and Security

The ethnic vision portrayed the diaspora Kazakhs, living in the adjacent territories (China and Mongolia had the largest concentration followed by Afghanistan, Pakistan, Iraq, Turkey and some in the West) as natural citizens of the new state and potentially more loyal than the majority of non-titular groups residing in Kazakhstan then. Certain members of the ruling Kazakh elite saw the solidarity emanating from a common or 'primordial' trait of ethnicity and kinship as more salient than the purported 'patriotism' of many Russian-speakers towards the Kazakhstani state. Initial declarations offered automatic and unconditional citizenship to ethnic Kazakhs desiring to return to their ancestral land. This was at a time when the nontitular groups were experiencing considerable anxieties over their legal and social status within the new republics. Though Kazakhstan did extend citizenship to all nationalities residing on its territories, the unconditional offer of citizenship to the diaspora was tantamount to granting them dual citizenship whereas demands by Russians for dual citizenship were not acceded to.

Kazakhstan made numerous pledges to extend equal citizenship and protect the rights of the Russian-speakers as Nazarbaev successfully portrayed himself as a promoter of ethnic solidarity and a protector of minorities. At the same time, the de facto nationalizing policies, particularly the grant of the state language status to Kazakh (and not to Russian) and the various measures to aid a regeneration of Kazakh culture and national symbols, produced considerable anxieties among the Russian-speakers about their future in the nationalizing state. These measures, together with the post-Soviet ethnic trends, resulted in a departure of almost two million Russian-speakers by the end of the 1990s. By the time Kazakhstan held its first post-independence census in 1999, the Russian share in the population had shrunk from 40 to 30 per cent and the total share of Russian-speaking groups (including Germans) had dropped to about 35 per cent from almost a half a decade earlier. Notwithstanding the official rhetoric of welcoming the Russians to stay, the ruling elites as a whole were not averse to the emigration of a critical mass of Russian-speakers and a rapid 'kazakhisation' of their demographic profile.

As Brubaker has shown, post-imperial ethnic unmixing a common phenomenon that informed the departure facilitated a relative and short-term process of ethnic homogenization, which in the interim sought to affirm the symbolic and normative ascendancy of the titular Kazakhs[7]. However, as next section shows, this has not brought to fruition the vision of a Kazakh national-state or (*natsional'noe gosudarstvo*) as anticipated by Kazakhstan' nationalist elites and its ideological and political establishment.

Settlement of the Kazakh diaspora

The total number of Kazakhs who have returned to their ethnic homeland since 1991 is estimated to be at least 750,000. Altynshash Zhaganova, the former head of the Committee on Migration, estimates the number to be about a million.[8] About two thirds of these have returned on the *oralman* quotas set by the government and the remaining ones, mainly from the former Soviet territories, have returned outside of the governmental quota. Altogether, between 1991 and 2007, a total of 165,861 families or about 651,299 Kazakh diaspora have returned on the basis of the *oralman* quotas set by the government.

The quotas for the *oralman* were highest during 1993–96: 10,000 families arrived in Kazakhstan in 1993. Of these the largest number, about 35 per cent, have come from Mongolia, followed by 8 per cent from Iran, 2 per cent from Turkey, 1.2 per cent from China, and 1 per cent from Afghanistan. The *oralman* quotas have been reduced to the range of 2,000–4,000 since then. The repatriation of Kazakhs from outside of CIS has practically reached its saturation point as the government has found it difficult to fill the lowered quotas set over the past two years. To be sure, any person of Kazakh origin is eligible to return to Kazakhstan and apply for Kazakhstani without availing of the quotas.

The families coming under the quota receive a one off settlement help of $5,000 (roughly $1,300 per person in the family), a plot of land, housing benefits, plus additional assistance for school-going children provided by local authorities. However. the returnees have a limited choice in determining the place of settlement. In the 1990s, the government settled the *oralman* in the Russian-dominated northern and eastern regions with a view to enhance the Kazakh share. Encountering numerous difficulties – from climatic to cultural-linguistic and economic – some *oralman* reportedly went back whereas others relocated to different parts, contravening the settlement guidelines.

Since 2003, the majority of returnee Kazakhs, those availing of the quotas as well as those coming outside of it, have been from Uzbekistan (61.5%), followed by 13.8 per cent from Mongolia, 8.5 per cent from Turkey and 7.7 per cent from China. Many from Uzbekistan and Russia have opted not to avail of the quota and the settlement subsidy. 'Rustem', an *oralman* from Tashkent who I interviewed in August 2008, reported having to deal with innumerable bureaucratic hurdles to prove that he was in fact a Kazakh ("my wife is Tatar, and they ask me 'why do you not have a Kazakh wife?'"). He wanted to live in Almaty, and not in Central or Northern Kazakhstan where several *oralman* have been settled. His logic was irrefutable: "I grew up in a sunny place, and have the right to choose to enjoy sunshine!"

The increase in the number of Kazakhs from Uzbekistan returning to Kazakhstan in recent years has generated speculation that many ethnic Uzbeks are reidentifying themselves as Kazakhs to take advantage of Kazakhstan's repatriation policy and move to Kazakhstan to better their economic prospects. Many in Kazakhstan would assert that 'Rustem' exemplifies an ethnic Uzbek seeking to recast himself as a Kazakh. It is common knowledge that ethnic groups in Central Asia inhabiting border regions where identity markers were multiple and fluid, had limited choice in placing themselves under a particular nationality category. Either they were forced to accept the particular nationality label or exerted their choice by selecting the nationality that allowed them to claim indigenous/titular status in the republic they were residing in.

About half to two thirds of labour migrants in Kazakhstan are from Uzbekistan. Between 1999 and 2008 57.6 per cent of migrants in Kazakhstan were from Uzbekistan. There are many joint businesses involving relatives and friends living in these two countries. Growing personal contacts between individuals across the borders have led to creation of informal networks. Kazakhs living in Uzbekistan play an important role in facilitating these ties. However, there is no agreement between the two governments that allow businesses to legally invite their partners and to recruit workers from the other country. Lacking opportunities to work and live legally in Kazakhstan, some citizens of Uzbekistan are procuring documentation that enables them to classify themselves as Kazakhs in order to settle in Kazakhstan.

Becoming Kazakhstani Citizens: Promise and Reality

Kazakhstan's bureaucratic structure and legal framework, shaped profoundly by Soviet-induced mechanisms of control and surveillance, places various obstacles to a speedy and dignified settlement and thus undermine the expectations of hospitality. In theory, those who were forced to flee during the Stalinist period time are automatically eligible for citizenship whereas other Kazakh diaspora desiring a return need to apply for settlement by making a petition addressed to President Nazarbaev. Attaining the entry to Kazakhstan for a member of Kazakh ethnicity is a fairly straightforward matter but the returnees then undergo a complicated process of attaining Kazakhstani citizenship.

The process of attaining documentation, *propiska* (residence permit), housing, passport, and obtaining the promised material assistance is a long and arduous one. A survey by Transparency International in Kazakhstan in 2005 showed that 64 percent of respondents were not aware of the laws dealing with their status. While the *oralman* are better informed today about the legal process of acquiring Kazakhstani citizenship, petty corruption has been reported in the various stages of formalizing the status as *oralman* and becoming a citizen: these range from apportioning of land for housing and farming; housing subsidies; sum granted for settlement and relocation, social welfare; registration, acquisition of the *oralman* status and gaining employment.[9] The Department of Migration and Demography has drawn considerable criticism for corruption and inefficiency in distributing these entitlements to the returnees. Low levels of literacy and limited awareness of legal rights among the *oralman* compound the problem. These hurdles have led some diaspora to return to their country of settlement whereas others, especially those moving from Russia, were made to rethink the decision to abandon their existing citizenship. Not only does the paperwork required for obtaining Kazakh citizenship remain complicated, the process of renouncing citizenship of Mongolia and Uzbekistan is also laden with bureaucratic complexities.

Kazakhstan's initial offer of citizenship to all Kazakhs residing abroad implied that the diaspora was eligible for dual citizenship. However, this offer turned out to have uncertain legal validity. China, Russia, Uzbekistan, and

Mongolia where a where significant numbers of Kazakh diaspora reside do not recognise dual citizenship. The returnee Kazakhs would have to renounce their existing citizenship upon becoming citizens of Kazakhstan – not an attractive proposition to a group that did not know Russian, the language that dominates Kazakhstan, and lacked facility in Cyrillic, the script in which Kazakh is written. Kazakhs, as well as Uighurs in China, use the Arabic script.

The symbolism of the citizenship pronouncement evaporated as a few years later Kazakhstan retracted the offer of dual citizenship granted to ethnic Kazakhs. The reasons were several. First, the offer was extended without looking into the practical and legal ramifications and without working out a proper legal base. Second, Russians residing in the territories of the former Soviet Union were also putting forth claims for dual citizenship at that time. In the early 1990s, Turkmenistan, Moldova formally allowed ethnic Russians to acquire Russian passports while maintaining the citizenship of these new states. Though Nazarbaev initially agreed to look into the demand favourably, Kazakh ruling elites were virtually unified in rejecting the claims of Russians for fear of nurturing the rise of a 'fifth column' within.

The lack of a clear programme facilitating the settlement of the *oralman* and the multifarious bureaucratic and administrative hurdles to speedy acquisition of Kazakhstani citizenship prolong the perception among them of being treated as second-tier citizens whose presence is desired for its numerical and symbolic value but is not enthusiastically welcomed. Kazakhs returning to their ancestral homeland see the provision of housing, job and other assistance as an entitlement as well as a part of traditional Kazakh hospitality.

A number of *oralman* have protested and seized lands and properties in the areas on the outskirts of the cities Almaty and Astana in defiance of the efforts by the officials to settle them in rural areas. On certain occasions, the returnees have found themselves competing with Kazakh rural migrants huddled in urban shantytowns in Almaty and Astana, who are also making claims for affordable housing. The latter complain of about being left outside of the land privatization process due to the absence of any legal help from the state and see themselves as more worthy of help than the returnee diaspora.

The state has faltered in absorbing the returnees into the labour market and creating an appropriate framework that facilitates their socialisation as Kazakhstan's citizens. Of 351,518 able-bodied population, about two thirds (211,154) have jobs whereas others are not in any regular employment.[10] Educational levels of the returnees remain lower than the national average, which is a further impediment to their effective absorption into the economy and labour market. In order to facilitate their entry into the field of higher education, 2 per cent of seats in the state universities have been allocated for the children of the *oralman*. However, it is too early to assess the impact of this provision.

Kazakhs living in Kazakhstan may share the trait of being a Kazakh – defined by the nomadic past and the centrality of genealogical knowledge – with their ethnic kin abroad. However, there is much that separates a Kazakh in Mongolia from one in China, Turkey or Afghanistan. A small stratum of Kazakhs in Mongolia is urbanised, well-versed in Russian language and integrated in Soviet values but the majority are engaged in livestock breeding and pastoral nomadic activity.

Kazakhs in China, who live in the Xinjiang Autonomous Region and are usually clubbed together with the Uighurs, form a distinctive group. While some may have close kin connections with Kazakhs across the border, most others are economically and culturally well integrated in the fabric of Chinese society. China's Kazakhs have higher educational and professional qualifications than the latter and have a greater proficiency in Chinese. The lack of knowledge of Russian, which remains the lingua franca across Kazakhstan, at least its urban areas, the lack of facility in the Cyrillic script (Uighurs and Kazakhs in China use the Arabic script to write their respective languages), and uncertain prospects of mobility have deterred China's Kazakhs from migrating to Kazakhstan. For a vast majority of them, the economic dynamism in China offers a better guarantee of prosperity and well-being than the prospect of return to their purported ethnic homeland.

Many urban Kazakhs see themselves as Eurasian and 'almost' as Europeans given their proximity to Russia and acceptance of Western culture. They display a greater socio-cultural affinity with members of Russian-speaking ethnic group than the returnees, whom they perceive as more traditional and provincial in outlook, lacking proper proficiency in Russian and possessing low level of educational and professional skills. Thus a separation between the urban and self-proclaimed 'Europeanised' ('sovietized') Kazakhs and their more 'traditional' ruling brethren is perpetuated within the nationalizing state framework. Questioning the pervasive stereotypes that portray the *oralman* as socially backward, culturally conservative and economically dependent on state subsidies, the representatives of the latter take pain to highlight their high level of culture, artistic talent and overall contribution to the society.[11]

The discovery in the early 1990s of one's kin in faraway places such as Germany, Norway and France introduced much euphoria and anticipation of their return. Kazakhs rejoiced at learning that their native language was spoken by their kin living in these faraway regions. Not only are the numbers of the Kazakh diaspora settled in the West extremely small, but a large number of them, especially those in Germany, UK, have been turkicised and adopted Turkish names and surnames.[12] Having established an economic, social and legal status for themselves in the West, few of these have had compelling incentives to return to Kazakhstan.

Scholars and experts involved in the formulation of policy towards the Kazakh returnees point out that the term *oralman* is derogatory. It refers to the animals separated from the herd and thus lost – a description that is seen as being both insulting as well as inaccurate. The government is debating the issue and plans to propose a new term.[13] The slow pace of integration and adjustment of the *oralman* to the mainstream society remains a matter of concern for the government. It is unclear what they are supposed to integrate into. Notwithstanding the continuing efforts by the state to manage and regulate ethnic relations and define an ethno-national ('Kazakh') and civil ('Kazakhstani) identity, there is no clear understanding on what these formulations mean. However they are defined, these conceptions of Kazakh or Kazakhstani identity are distant from the experience of *oralman*, particularly from Mongolia, reared in Kazakh language milieu, whose life experience is shaped by a nomadic life-style and remains anchored within the structure of *aul* and clan. The most ardent champions of the rights of the returnees and their rapid assimilation into the society are the Kazakh nationalists, who enjoy symbolic recognition but no substantive power and are marginalized within the existing configuration of power at the centre.

Israel and Germany, in that order, are two relatively successful examples of states which have well-entrenched policies of ethnic repatriation and integration of the co-ethnics through massive financial investment and socialization as citizens. Israel's success in integrating returnee Jews can be attributed to an intensive and compulsory military training, the teaching of Hebrew and socialisation into being an Israeli whose identity as a Jew is indisputably anchored in the memory and trauma of the holocaust. Germany's long tradition of descent-based approach to citizenship has encouraged any person able to prove his/her German roots – an *Aussiedler* – to qualify for German citizenship. At the same time, the German state has encountered resistance among the *Aussiedler*, especially the older Soviet-reared generation, to learning German and embracing the liberal multiculturalism that the state has actively sought to promote. In contrast to these two states, Kazakhstan has invested far fewer resources into the integration of the returnees through effective citizenship socialisation and socio-economic protection.

Kazakhstan's Demographic and Labour Needs

As the discussion above has shown, Kazakhstan' migration policy has been defined by the objective of facilitating a return of the Kazakh diaspora. There were two key challenges that Kazakhstan's policymakers failed to anticipate and thus take adequate measures to plan. The first one was the renewal of demographic base. Demography is a vital national asset. While overpopulation and population density have put pressures on land and natural resources and become stumbling block to development and state security (in Bangladesh, Rwanda, Congo, Pakistan, parts of India), sparse population over a vast territories of land also portends to be a developmental and state-building challenge. The arrival of about a million *oralman* has not adequately filled the demographic void left by the outmigration of almost two million Russian-speakers (including Germans) over the past two decades, the steady fall in birth rate among Kazakhs, and the propensity on the part of the urbanised and privileged Kazakhs to study and work abroad.

The second shortcoming was the failure to anticipate the manner in which Kazakhstan's economic growth would define its need for labour and specialists. Kazakhstan's GDP is larger than the combined one of the remaining four Central Asian states and its per capita earnings are also highest in the Central Asian region. It is aspiring to join 50 most competitive economies in the world in 2010 and enter the group of top five oil exporters by 2015. The economic upturn has led to the booming of certain sectors of the economy – particularly oil, banking, telecommunications, construction, and service. This has generated the need for a variety of skilled and unskilled workers in newly emerging as sectors of the economy – oil, energy, construction, services – as well as in well as in traditional one such as agriculture. The Ministry of Interior Affairs estimates that Kazakhstan will need about

500,000 foreign workers by the year 2015 to fill the labour deficit.[14]

Kazakhstan's ruling elites, government officials and law and order authorities have tended to see the entry of labour migrants as a nation-building challenge and a security concern, which is consistent with the securitization framework that shaped its perception of the nontitular minorities in the 1990s. The debates in the media as well as policy discussions centre on issues such as establishment of effective border control and visa regimes, introduction of quotas and other restrictions on arrival of migrants, efficient process of registration of foreigners. There is little discussion of the economic and demographic benefits of migration to the economy or the consequences of a growing depopulation trends.

About 9000 foreign citizens and 73,700 from CIS have been officially registered as migrant workers.[15] International experts estimate that some 75 per cent of foreign labour migrants in Kazakhstan, constituting about half a million, were working without proper work authorization in 2008, and are varyingly categorized as 'illegal', 'irregular', or 'temporary' migrants.[16] Though often referred to as 'illegal' (*nelegal'nye*) migrants, they are in fact migrants with unregulated legal status, a term proposed by International Organization of Migration (IOM) and International Labour Organization (ILO). The highest number of migrants is from Uzbekistan, currently estimated to be 400,000 to 600,000. The number of migrants from Kyrgyzstan was estimated to be 150,000 to 180,000 during 2006–2007 and could be higher.[17] While almost three fourths of the Kyrgyz migrants opt to go to Russia, the share of those working as seasonal workers or migrants in Kazakhstan is rising. Although the financial crisis has halted most construction projects in both Kazakhstan and Russia and reduced the need for labour migrants from the neighbouring Central Asian states, there is no conclusive evidence that it has led to a significant departure of the migrants. It is far more likely that they have been absorbed in other sectors of the economy.

The migrants are working predominantly in construction and retail, agriculture and housing services, employed in what is known as the 3-D jobs ('dirty, dangerous and degrading') which are shunned by the local people because the pay is too low. The availability of foreign 'undocumented' migrant labour is a main reason why pay-scales for these jobs, which require a steady supply of workers, remain low.

These migratory movements are not simply triggered by the growing economic disparities within the central Eurasian region: they are also reproducing these disparities. Boosted by dynamics within the region and forces of globalization and transnationalism, they undercut the nationalizing and homogenizing policies pursued by the national ruling establishment during the first decade of their independence.

Conclusion

The analysis in this chapter has drawn attention to the enormous challenges that policies of ethnic repatriation encounter within a globalizing framework in which regional and transnational factors, rather than national policies. The efforts to boost its demographic base by bringing in Kazakh diaspora from neighbouring states of Central Asia as well as from Mongolia, Afghanistan, Iran, Iraq, Turkey, and China have reached a saturation point as very few Kazakhs from outside of the CIS are availing of the repatriation offer. Its population of about 15 million is unlikely to grow further through natural increase and migration is the only solution to regenerating population levels.

Kazakhstan found it difficult to economically absorb and culturally integrate the diaspora returnees and the separation between the titular Kazakhs and the returnees remains pronounced. At the same time, the growing pool of labour migrants from the neighbouring Central Asian states (and some from beyond), face enormous obstacles in working legally and attaining social acceptance despite their substantial contribution to the country's economic growth and service provision. Furthermore, as a result of the shared Soviet experience, the labour migrants from Central Asia fit into the Kazakhstani society more easily in cultural and social terms than the ethnic Kazakh returnees from outside the former Soviet republics.

Kazakhstan's migration policy is hamstrung by the ethnonationalist logic, which offered a key rationale for launching the policy of repatriation of the *oralman* to their ethnic homeland. Multiethnic Kazakhstan is a site of contestation between the ethnonational formulation of the nation state in which membership into the nation/nation-state is defined primarily by one's ethnic origin and the challenges of transnational mobility generated by globalization as well as Kazakhstan's geographical location in the Eurasian landmass. The problems encountered in the integration of the *oralman* in the fabric of Kazakhstani society and state apparatus show that ethnic repatriation targets and policies are very difficult to achieve in the absence of a democratic notion of citizenship or a shared vision of national ideology.

Notes and References

1. The concept of a post-Soviet 'nationalizing state' is described by Rogers Brubaker in the chapter, 'Nationalizing states in the old "New Europe" – and the new' in *Nationalism Reframed: Nationhood and the National Question in the New Europe*, Cambridge: Cambridge University Press, 1996: 79–106.
2. A fuller elaboration of this argument is in Bhavna Dave, *Kazakhstan: Ethnicity, Language and Power*, London: Routledge, 2007. See Chapter 6 "Disempowered Minorities" in particular.
3. The forced settlement (collectivization) of the Kazakh nomads executed under the Stalinist regime during the late 1920s to early 1930s resulted in a widespread famine, deaths, dislocation and displacement of Kazakhs. About one fourth to forty percent of Kazakhs are estimated to have died as a result.
4. Makash Tatimov, *Haliq nama: san men sana*, Almaty: Zhazushi, 1992.
5. The results of Kazakhstan's national census held in 2009 have not yet been made official.
6. Alexander C. Diener, "Kazakhstan's Kin State Diaspora: Settlement Planning and the Oralman Dilemma", *Europe-Asia Studies*, Vol. 57, No. 2 (Mar., 2005), pp. 327–348. Of these estimated 4.1 million, at least 750,000 have already repatriated to Kazakhstan.
7. Brubaker, "Nationalism Reframed".
8. http://rus.azattyq.org/articleprintview/1958431.html, accessed on 19 February, 2010.
9. http://www.enbek.kz/migration/migr_rusdetail.php?recordID=36&mintrud=1, accessed on 20 December 2008.
10. *Ibid.*
11. http://rus.azattyq.org/articleprintview/1958431.html, accessed on 19 February, 2010.
12. Author's personal interactions with ethnic Kazakh diaspora residing in Germany and England.
13. Author's conversations with Ziabek Kabyldinov, an *oralman* returnee from Omsk and a dean at the Eurasian University in Astana, August 2008.
14. "Migrantov stanet bol'she," ["There will be more migrants"], *Kursiv*, (28 February 2008). http://www.kursiv.kz

15. M. Aisberg, "Vozvrashchenie bludnogo migranta", *Express K*, no. 33, (22 February 2008).
16. *Kazakhstanskaia Pravda,* 25 August 2008.
17. Interviews with members of International Organization for Migration (IOM) in Almaty, 11 August 2008.

Contributors

Bhavna Dave, Department of Politics and International Studies, SOAS, University of London.

Boris V. Bazarov, Director of the Institute for Mongolian, Buddhist and Tibetan Studies of the Siberian Branch of RAS (IMBTS SB RAS), Ulan Ude, Russia; Chairman the Presidium of the Buryat Scientific Center of SB RAS, Ulan Ude.

Gulnara Mendikulova, Director, Research Center on Diaspora Studies, the World Association of the Kazakhs, Almaty, Republic of Kazakhstan;Chief, the Department of Complex Problems of International Affairs, Deputy Editor of International Journal SHYGYS (Orient) at the Institute of Oriental Studies, Ministry of Education and Science, Republic of Kazakhstan (IOS MES RK) (Almaty, KZ).

Homeswar Goswami, Retired Professor, Department of Economics, Dibrugarh University, Dibrugarh, Assam, India.

Jayanta Kumar Ray, Coordinator, Documentation Centre, Maulana Azad Museum, Maulana Abul Kalam Azad Institute of Asian Studies, Kolkata, India.

Kamilla Sheryazdanova, Professor of International Relations Department, Eurasian National University named after L.N. Gumilyev, Astana, Kazakhstan.

Nandini Bhattacharya, Associate Professor, Calcutta Girls' College, Kolkata, India.

P.L. Dash, Professor of Eurasian Studies, University of Mumbai, India.

List of Russian Translation

The following article was translated from its original Russian version to English by Vslevod Bashkuev, Research Fellow, IMBT, SB RAS, Ulan Ude and Susmita Bhattacharya, Fellow, Maulana Abul Kalam Azad Institute of Asian Studies, Kolkata.

- B.V. Bazarov and N.I. Atanov, *New Tendencies in East Asian Geopolitics*

Index